The New Covenant
of Bill Clinton
and Al Gore

Neo-pagan Fundamentalism
and the
New Politics

THE NEW COVENANT OF BILL CLINTON AND AL GORE

Neo-pagan Fundamentalism
and the
New Politics

John Barela

Mark 4 Publications, Inc.
10977 East 23rd Street
Tulsa, Oklahoma, 74129

The New Covenant of Bill Clinton and Al Gore

Neo-pagan Fundamentalism and the New Politics

Copyright © 1992 by John Barela. Published by

Mark 4 Marketing, Inc.
10977 East 23rd Street
Tulsa, OK 74129

Scripture quotations are from the King James Version of The Holy Bible.

Cover design by Texe Marrs

Acknowledgments

A book such as this is never possible without being exposed to the varied insights of many wonderful Christian friends. We are indebted to those who have shared their personal research.

I especially want to thank my wife, Sharon, who has truly been an "help-meet" for me and the ministry God has given us. Her editorial work on the manuscript has been invaluable.

A special word of thanks is also given to Berit Kjos for her assistance in sharing information, and allowing us to quote excerpts from her outstanding book, *"Under the Spell of Mother Earth."* God has given her great insights into the neo-pagan environmental movement. Berit also introduced us to Craig Rucker of CFACT who provided us with information he is using to expose the big lie of the environmental movement.

We know that one day, God will acknowledge the faithfulness of each of these dedicated people to the praise of His glory.

Forward

The revelations in this book are disturbing. Especially because they come from John Barela, one of America's most noted authorities on the New Age movement and pagan philosophies. Governor Bill Clinton and his vice presidential running mate, Senator Al Gore, are promising the people of the United States a New Covenant. But as the author so convincingly documents, in fact, their promised New Covenant is not new at all. Indeed, it is shown to be old, rather ancient, and alarmingly un-Christian.

It is apparent that Bill Clinton and Al Gore, while claiming to be "born-again Christians," embrace philosophies and viewpoints diametrically opposed to traditional Christianity. As John Barela reveals, these two men, who would occupy America's highest elective offices, are not only social liberals, but spiritually, they are models and mentors, promoting a pagan agenda certain to push our nation toward corruption and destruction, rather than towards healing and harmony.

Al Gore's own bestselling book, *Earth in the Balance: Ecology and the Human Spirit,* demonstrates that he is a fervent supporter of Hinduism, Buddhism, Native American spiritism and other Earth-centered religions. In fact, in the book, while applauding gurus and shamans from the East, he is highly critical of many Christians, especially those who are conservative and pro-Bible.

Al Gore indicates in his book that he is much more in tune with today's radical feminists who are teaching the old witchcraft religion of the Mother Earth Goddess than he is with the average American Christian. Moreover, he professes that his ultimate goal is a "New Faith for the future," a faith that, on examination, turns out to be a warmed-over mixture of New Age faddism, radical environmentalism, and contemporary paganism.

Meanwhile, Bill Clinton, who so often proudly points to his own Southern Baptist heritage is publicly opposed to almost everything that Baptists stand for. For example, most Baptists abhor the carnage of abortion, but Clinton claims that it's a woman's free choice to maim and kill her unborn child. He has also signalled his support of the bizarre agenda of activist lesbian and homosexual organizations.

The tragic fact is that Bill Clinton and Al Gore have bought into the destructive life-denying values of pagan, Mother Earth philosophies. As a result, these two men are outsiders to the kind of morality and integrity historically endorsed by America's greatest national leaders, from George Washington and Abraham Lincoln to Teddy Roosevelt.

Apparently, Bill Clinton and Al Gore care more for "Mother Earth" than they do for individual dignity and the sanctity of human life. And philosophically, their views are closer to those of the Dalai Lama of Tibetan Buddhism and failed socialist Mikhail Gorbachev than with our great Christian leaders of the past who made America into the most caring, most God-fearing, and most prosperous nation on planet Earth.

I am grateful to John Barela for exposing the harmful views of Bill Clinton and Al Gore to the light of truth and American experience. My prayer is that millions of concerned Americans will read and heed the cautionary warnings in this book.

Texe Marrs
Austin, Texas

INTRODUCTION

This book is not a partisan treatise. Whether you are Democrat or Republican, you must be alerted to the dangers that lie ahead. As you will see from documented evidence that follows, there is a "hidden agenda" behind many of the plans and proposals made by Bill Clinton and Al Gore.

We do not speculate. We quote from their own writings, speeches, and from interviews printed in popular periodicals and journals. One of our most revealing sources of information is Al Gore's new best-selling book, *"Earth in the Balance: Ecology and the Human Spirit."*

Our desire is to present the documented evidence, then let you make up your own mind based on fact. After researching for this book, we have come to some startling conclusions based on these facts. We do not ask you to agree, but simply to do justice to yourself and those you care about by examining the documentation presented.

Eminent dangers presently confront us: (1.) *If Mr. Gore's system of occult spirituality is followed, Christi-*

anity would be eradicated and America would make a quantum leap into the occult New Age, One-World religious system. (2.) *If his economic policies involving the redistribution of our wealth and resources are followed, the United States will be catapulted backward to the status of a Third World country.*

Al Gore is an avid environmentalist. Environmentalists (deep ecologists) are gaining more power each day. Are all their goals pure? What dark secrets are locked in the obscure verbage of the proposals made at the recent Earth Summit? What are Bill Clinton's and Al Gore's plans for America as President, and Vice President? Although it may serve as somewhat of a "shock treatment," I strongly encourage you to read this book from cover to cover, then let the documentation speak for itself - *THE WORST IS YET TO COME!*

From the Horse's Mouth

An article which appeared in the August 13, 1992 issue of *The Wallstreet Journal* is entitled, *"Worried Memo: Dems Ponder Green Gore."* It quoted a copy of a memo sent by Democratic National Committee staffer Jonathan Sallet to the Clinton campaign, alerting them to some of the problems that could arise if people were to read Al Gore's new book, *Earth in the Balance: Ecology and the Human Spirit* (referred to as "EITB" in the text of the memo:

Remember, this memo was written by a Democratic staff member to Democratic leaders so that they would have advance warning of potential problems that could arise because of Gore's book. His intent was to prepare them in case these issues were to surface during the campaign. We quote:

""This memorandum will list the basic thematic attacks on *"Earth in the Balance."* There are, of course, a series of other, technical, objections that can be made to the book.. . . .

'Specific Areas of Thematic Attack.' After our conversation, it seems to me that the basic attacks on EITB will fall in the following three categories:

Al is not qualified to be vice-president.

- *He has no principles. He admits that he has voted for programs in which he does not believe (EITB at 340), has changed his campaign tactics merely to suit the advice of political consultants (EITB at 8-9, at 167-169), and uses products that he simultaneously criticizes as being harmful to the environment (EITB at 15).*

- *He is a classic Washington insider, who has been trained since an early age to tailor his views to what he thinks the voters want to hear, not what he really believes (EITB at 9, 13, 15).*

- *He is a weak figure who, as he admits, feels "paralyzed" (EITB at 2), who has suffered the throes of a mid-life crisis (EITB at 14), and who doesn't even know what he thinks (EITB at 13).*

- *He's apparently guilt-ridden about the role of men in society (EITB at 213) and, perhaps as a result of his own weakness, believes that America as a whole is psychologically dysfunctional (EITB at 230-31).*

- *He is a hypocrite who urges [the need to stabilize] populaton growth on others while revering his own large family (EITB at 307).*

- *He is a bad scientist, who doesn't care enough to get his facts straight. The fact is, we can't be certain that global warming or the level of CO_2 or* even the changes in the ozone layer pose a threat as burdensome as the costs of Al Gore's proposals. **Al is a radical environmentalist who wants to change the very fabric of America.**

- **He criticizes America for being America** - *a place where people enjoy the benefits of an advanced standard of living (EITB at 147, 156, 161, 308),*

- **He has no sense of proportion:** *He equates the failure to recycle aluminum cans with the Holocaust - an equation that parodies the former and dishonors the latter (EITB at 177-78, 275).*

- *He is a Luddite who* **holds the naive view that technology is evil and wants to abolish automobiles** *(EITB at 206, 318).*

- **He believes that our civilization, itself, is evil** *(because it is, in his words, "addicted to the consumption of the earth") (EITB at 220). If Al Gore has his way, we would give up America's jobs and destroy the economy.*

- **All he wants to do is raise a host of taxes,** *including carbon taxes, pollution charges, a "Virgin Materials Fee,"* **and a gasoline tax.** *(EITB at 273, 348-49).*

- **He is a big spender** *who thinks that we have to support the environmental programs of the entire world. (EITB 297, 304, 317).*

- **Wants to stop or retard economic growth.** *(EITB at 297, 300-310, 341, 342, 345).*

- **Wants to destroy the automotive industry, and a lot of jobs along with it.** *(EITB at 3[2]5).*

- **Favors the spotted owl over jobs.** *(EITB at 121).*

- **Wants to give away American technology**

Table of Contents

CHAPTER ONE

THE NEW COVENANT OF BILL CLINTON AND AL GORE

Bill Clinton, Democratic candidate for President, in his acceptance speech introduced a new campaign theme - "The New Covenant" of Bill Clinton and Al Gore.

Strongly aware of the cry for change brought to the fore by the landslide of support for Ross Perot, they are attempting to wed the connotation of "change," that magnetized Perot supporters, to the biblical terminology, "New Covenant," to attract support from the "middle" and "religious right." They now want to "be all things to all men." His strategic move, however, backfired in an angry cry from the "religious right" he is trying so desperately to woo.

USA Today, July 21, 1992 reported that "Two well-known evangelists, both supporters of Republican issues, say Democrat Bill Clinton misquoted the Bible in his acceptance speech last week. Clinton, a Southern Baptist, cited several Biblical passages in his speech, including use of a *"new covenant"* as his campaign theme.

"TV evangelist. . .Pat Robertson charged that Clinton only partially quoted Biblical passages and failed to mention their full religious contexts.

"Robertson, speaking on his *700 Club* show. . .noted that Clinton's call for a "new covenant" with voters - mentioned 10 times in last week's speech - was a term used by Jesus as he poured wine, representing his blood, for apostles at the Last Supper.

"'If it isn't blasphemous, it certainly borders on it,' said Robertson, who cited Clinton's pro-choice stance on abortion. 'This, to me, is extremely dangerous. . .Don't come up with pseudo-Christianity to mask what you're doing.'

Jerry Falwell released a statement showing his disdain, ". . .'misquoting and manipulating the Holy Scripture for political purposes should be offensive to millions of Americans. . .It is certainly a more significant error than the much-publicized misspelling of potato.'"

Why would these two men consider it blasphemy to refer to Clinton and Gore's campaign slogan as *"The New Covenant?"* Could it be that they are privy to the truth about what Gore describes as the "spiritual faith" he is clinging to - to carry us into the next century?

The Faith of Al Gore

In order to help us understand what Gore means when he refers to his "faith," to "spirituality," and to a "new covenant," let's look at some of the people he esteems, quotes, and projects to possess the insights to lead us into this new "spiritual" era.   In his new bestselling book, *Earth in the Balance, Ecology and the Human Spirit*, he refers to Teilhard de Chardin, *"a Catholic theologian,"* in a manner that would "suggest" that there are "some Christians" who have a degree of enlightenment. He fails to inform us, however, that this Catholic theologian/archaeologist had been *EXCOMMUNICATED* from the Roman Catholic Church and is a *SPIRITUAL EVOLUTIONIST.*

Gore quotes Fr. de Chardin on page 263 as saying, "The fate of mankind, as well as of religion, depends upon the emergence of *A NEW FAITH IN THE FUTURE.*" Al Gore then goes on to say that, *"Armed with SUCH A FAITH, we might find it possible to RESANCTIFY the earth."* (emphasis ours)

"Sanctify," is a religious term, but what does Gore actually mean when he uses the term "re-sanctify?" Is he telling us that humans have the power to sanctify - *make holy* - the earth that God placed under a curse ? (Genesis 3:14-19)

21

Or is he implying that the earth already is sacred, but that our Western, Christian culture has dulled our awareness. Al Gore And Pantheism

Now we must restore our own consciousness of that universal sacredness - and through our own adjusted consciousness, restore nature to its true state? The latter statement seems to fit into Gore's pagan persuasions and joins his philosophy to that of contemporary New Age leaders.

In contrast to Biblical teaching, Gore views all parts of nature as sacred. By misinterpreting a Biblical passage in Genesis 11, he writes that ". . .God's covenant, made not only with Noah, but with 'all living creatures,' again affirm[s] *the sacredness of creation.*" (p. 245)

This statement matches his message on page 265, where he affirms his pantheistic view with an *incredible distortion* of the Biblical God: *the idea that ALL OF GOD is in ALL PARTS OF NATURE:*

"My understanding of how God is manifest in the world can be best conveyed through the metaphor of the *hologram.* . .I believe that the image of the Creator, which sometimes seems so faint in the tiny corner of CREATION each of us beholds, is nonetheless *present IN ITS ENTIRETY."*

Contemporary disciples of *neo-paganism,* traditional *occultism,* the *New Age movement* and much of the *human potential movement* share a common trust in the mind's power to alter physical realities. "Consciousness" is one of the buzzwords that communicate this persuasion. Thus by choosing the state of our own consciousness, we can direct the evolution of the earth and make it sacred - *perfect by the single act of believing it into being.*

Marilyn Ferguson, a leading New Age spokesperson, in her book, *The Aquarian Conspiracy, Personal and Social Transformation in the 1980s,* is also on a quest for a *"dramatic cultural shift"* (The terms used to describe Ferguson's proposals by the World Future Society). Is it coincidence that she also cites the ideals of Teilhard de Chardin, Gore's inspirational source, in her book? "In every age, said scientist-philosopher Pierre Teilhard de Chardin, man has proclaimed himself at a turning point in history. 'And to a certain extent, as he is advancing on a rising spiral, he has not been wrong. But there are moments when this impression of *TRANS-FORMATION* becomes accentuated and IS thus PARTICULARLY JUSTIFIED.' (emphasis ours)

"Teilhard prophesied the phenomenon central to this book: *A CONSPIRACY OF MEN AND WOMEN* whose *NEW PERSPECTIVE* would trigger a *CRITICAL CONTAGION OF CHANGE.* (emphasis ours)

"Throughout history virtually all efforts to *REMAKE SOCIETY* began by altering its outward form and organization. It was assumed that rational social structure could produce harmony by a system of rewards, punish-

23

ments, manipulations of power. But the periodic attempts to achieve a just society. . .seem to have been thwarted. . .and now what? (emphasis ours)

"*The Aquarian Conspiracy* represents the Now What.

"Taking a broader view of history and a deeper measure of NATURE, *The Aquarian Conspiracy* is a *different kind of revolution,* with different revolutionaries. It looks to the *TURNABOUT IN CONSCIOUSNESS OF A CRITICAL NUMBER OF INDIVIDUALS, ENOUGH TO BRING ABOUT A RENEWAL OF SOCIETY."* (emphasis ours)

Gore calls for a *"re-sanctification,"* Ferguson calls for a *"transformation,"* a *"renewal."* It all sounds wonderful - until you look a little further and find out what these pious ideologies entail.

CHAPTER TWO

LET'S WEIGH THE EVIDENCE CLINTON AND GORE - BAPTISTS???

The Bible cautions us, *"Let no man deceive you by any means: For that day shall not come, except there come a falling away first. . . .And for this cause God shall send them strong delusion, that they should believe a lie."* II Thes. 2:3, 11

Interestingly, Bill Clinton and Al Gore both claim to be Baptists. *In Earth in the Balance: Ecology and the Human Spirit* - a massive and controversial volume born out of trauma and transformation - Al Gore claims to be a Baptist and occasionally uses words and concepts that simulate evangelical Christianity. As we point out, his view of our nation's problems and his suggested solutions are as contrary to Baptist theology as occult spiritism is to Biblical prayer.

Let's weigh the evidence. Baptists are Baptist because they hold to a certain, specific theology - that is what separates them from other denominations, sects and cults. If a person identifies himself with the Baptist group, it should hold true that they also identify with, and hold to, Baptist theology. We have been examining the actual statements of both Bill Clinton and Al Gore, and we have yet to identify anything even vaguely similar to Baptist theology in their personally stated beliefs.

GORE'S RELIGIOUS FAITH
A NEW AGE PARADIGM SHIFT

New Age Theology Defined

In order to better understand Gore's new theology, we must give some background information on "New Age" theology, so that you will be able to identify it for yourself, when you see it in Gore's writings. We will define what we describe as New Age theology as opposed to Baptist theology. The view described as "Christian," given in the following quote from *Basic Principles of New Age Thought* by Dr. John Eidsmoe, follows the exact tenets of theology held by Baptists. Examine both theologies closely, and in the following documentation, compare both theologies with the statements and writings of Al Gore - then you make your own decision as to whether he is a Baptist or possibly "former" Baptist, turned New Ager.

"New Age theology parallels Christian theology in some respects. Both teach that man has fallen from his original state, and both offer a way of salvation.

"The Bible teaches that man was originally created in an ideal state. . .in an ideal environment. . . .But he chose to sin by. . .disobeying God. . ." As a result of his disobedience, man, along with the entire creation, fell under the curse of God. "As a result the earth is not the perfect environment it once was. . . ." Another consequence of sin is that "man is unable to have fellowship with God, because while God still continues to love mankind, He is a God of righteousness and He will not tolerate sin in his presence. . . .

"In a sense, the New Ager too sees the problem in terms of man's estrangement from God. But in the New Age view, *nature is God*, and the problem is man's alienation from nature. . .the New Age movement does not believe in sin, at least not in any traditional biblical sense of the term. As Shakti Gawain explains, 'The truth about this earth is that it is an infinitely good, beautiful, nourishing place to be. The only 'evil' comes from lack of understanding of this truth. . . .'

According to New Age theology, ". . .the problem is lack of consciousness about the environment, or over population, or modern technology. . .we are all part of a global ecological community. *Some even say the problem is traditional Christians who believe they have been created separate and distinct from nature instead of having evolved through nature.* One New Age writer has even suggested *that the current environmental crisis is the Earth Mother rejecting and throwing off the mandate that the Judeo-Christian God gave to man to exercise dominion over the earth.. . .*

27

"Just as Christianity and the New Age both see the problem as man's estrangement from God, so Christianity and the New Age both see the solution as coming back to God. However, Christians believe man is unable [in and of himself] to come back to God, because man is corrupted by sin. So God took the initiative and. . .He took upon Himself human flesh in the Person of Jesus Christ. . . .As the incarnate Son of God, Jesus Christ died upon the Cross for the sin of the world, thereby paying the penalty [of sin] for us. . . ." and reconciling us to God.

"In the New Age view, the solution is to come back to God. But *God is nature, so getting back to God means getting back to nature.* And that is primarily man's responsibility, because man is the most highly conscious part of nature.

"In general. . .the New Age movement views the earth not simply as a rocky planet on which various life forms make their homes. Rather, the earth herself is a living, vibrant organism, *to be worshiped as God. So the earth is often capitalized as Planet Earth, or Spaceship Earth, or the Earth Mother, or the Mother Goddess.*"

THE PARADIGM SHIFT OF AL GORE

Gore says he is a Baptist, so we must assume that he may still be under the illusion that he can claim that name. But could it be that he has undergone a "*paradigm shift*" that has subtly and totally eradicated his former theology? When we read his writings, there is only one conclusion we can draw according to the vast weight of clear, documented evidence.

U.S. News and World Report, July 20, 1992, says Gore is not the same man who campaigned for president so feverishly in 1988. It took his son's horrible accident to get Gore *"centered."* "Centered" is a rather frightening term to Baptists and other Bible believing Christians because it carries with it an overtone of New Ageism - it is a term often used in New Age theology, never in Christian theology. But let's not make judgments merely on terminology, let's thoroughly examine Gore's own statements to get at the "truth."

The article told of a painful experience in the parking lot of Baltimore's Memorial Stadium when Gore's 6-year-old son "darted out of his father's grasp-and into the postgame traffic. A car struck young Albert. . . ." Devastated, Gore spent 30 days in the hospital with his young son as he fought for life.

Gore says, "For the next month, my wife, Tipper, and I stayed in the hospital consumed with the struggle to restore his body and spirit. And for me *SOMETHING CHANGED* in a fundamental way. I don't think my son's brush with death was solely responsible, although that was the *CATALYST.* But I had also just lost a presidential campaign; moreover, I had just turned forty years old. I was, in a sense, *vulnerable to the change that sought me out in the middle of my life. . .*" (emphasis ours)

The New Psychology - Road to Transformation

An article in *Time Magazine*, July 20, 1992 provides us with further insight. Besides his son's brush with death, Gore shares in his book, what *OTHER FORCES* helped *ALTER* his world view. The article reveals, "What Gore does not mention in the book - and did not, in fact, publicly reveal until last week - is the pivotal role psychological counseling played in helping him and his wife."

While Psychology and Psychiatry have provided some valuable information about human behavior and medical treatment of neurological disorders, they have also opened the door to a flood of occult influences. Carl Jung, one of Gore's sources of information, studied Tibetan Buddhism, practiced tantric yoga, and received much of the "wisdom" that has directed modern psychology by channeling (occult spiritism) his spirit guide, Philemon.

There is a dangerous new trend in psychological counseling that seems to fit right in with what we hear Al Gore saying. A magazine entitled, *Common Boundary Between Spirituality and Psychotherapy*, perfectly describes our premise. *"The New Frontier Of Psychotherapy Is Spirituality*. And *Common Boundary* is at the forefront of this new movement. . . .we. . .track down new perspectives on clinical issues, chart professional developments and trends, stimulate dialogue and discussion, and support the integration of spiritual values and principles in the practice of psychotherapy.

". . .helping psychotherapists, pastoral counselors, and others in the healing and helping professions sort out the spiritual dimensions of psychotherapy and the psychological aspects of spiritual growth.

"By investigating transpersonal, Jungian and humanistic psychology; pastoral counseling; consciousness-expanding disciplines such as meditation, contemplation and dreamwork; and healing tools such as biofeedback, imagery. . .we provide a comprehensive overview of the concerns, pitfalls, techniques and people involved in *TRANSFORMATIONAL* (emphasis ours) processes."

As we try to understand the different elements that have combined to shape Al Gore's philosophies and beliefs, here, we find another clue that fits into the emerging picture. In fact, Tipper Gore received a psychology degree from Boston University. Later she earned a master's degree.

There is no way we can reconcile the occult views of Carl Jung, to Baptist theology or Christian theology in general. Nor do Baptists endorse psychological *"therapies"* such as *"consciousness-expanding,"* *"meditation,"* *"dreamwork,"* *"biofeedback,"* and *"imagery."*

Notice that they describe these psychological exercises as *"transformational."* Where have we seen this "buzzword" before - *The Aquarian Conspiracy*? If you have studied the New Age movement, you are aware of the major role New Age teaching techniques have played in psychological counseling. If you are not a student of the New Age, you may not be aware that one of the roots of New Age thought is modern psychology or vice versa.

The New Age movement has many faces, and they are as varied as the masks at a masquerade party. Whatever your concern or problem, it dawns the mask that will attract you - psychology, spirituality, the environment, health, you name it. *The danger is that all roads in the New Age lead to the same destination - a "spiritual" awakening, or initiation.*

The promises and goals of the New Age environmentalist appear, on the surface, to be wonderful. They parallel the same aspirations of every good American citizen - a clean, healthy environment - green trees, clean air, preservation of the natural beauty that God Himself created. But when we dig a little deeper, we see its roots are, in fact, *"spiritual"* (as Al Gore so clearly points out), and they tap into a different form of spirituality than would appear on the surface - *occult spirituality.*

Most New Agers probably started out most innocently, with idealistic dreams, just as Eve, in the Garden of Eden. Then came the serpent, so beautiful, so seductive, and so convincing - but the serpent was *"not what he appeared to be."* Eve did not see the true person of Satan until she took the bite of the luscious fruit. After it was too late, her eyes were opened, and she saw, for the first time, what evil was, and the consequences of following evil counsel.

This is the reason that the Bible continually warns us, *"But evil men and seducers shall wax worse and worse,*

deceiving, and being deceived. But continue thou in the things which thou hast learned. . .knowing of whom thou hast learned them" (II Timothy 3:13-14). Revelation 18:23 describes the deception as being so great that *"by thy sorceries were all nations deceived."*

We know that you do not have to be an evil person to be deceived. Most of the time "good people" who only want "good things" for themselves and their loved ones fall prey under the right set of circumstances. . . .

Al Gore suddenly found himself a victim of deep pain, challenged by three major crises confronting him almost simultaneously - he had just lost a presidential campaign, turned 40, and now his son's very life lay hanging in the balance. He saw his son hovering between life and death. Could he have felt the need for a positive experience in his life - a need to build, construct, to do something significant in an attempt to turn back the tide of devastation that was sweeping over his fragile world?

It was during this vulnerable and traumatic time in his life that Al Gore was "transformed." According to *Time Magazine*, July 20, 1992, "'It was a terrible jolt for Al, *a defining moment,*'" says a longtime friend. 'Al hasn't been the same since.'" Al says, "*It completely changed my outlook on life.*'"

A New Al Gore

It was while spending his time in an office in the hospital that Al Gore began to write the environmental book that has catapulted him into the political limelight and made him a "PC" (politically correct) one-world, New Age darling.

Gore writes in his book, *Earth In The Balance: Ecology And The Human Spirit*, "The more deeply I search for the roots of the global crisis, the more I am convinced that it is [caused] by an inner crisis that is, for lack of a better word, spiritual."

WHAT DOES HE MEAN BY SPIRITUAL?

We know that he evidently does not mean spiritual as referring to Christianity and the Holy Spirit, because this would not be PC, or "politically correct," and as we have seen by the slant of publicity concerning Al Gore, he is one man who is now considered to be PC. As we read further, the article leaves no doubt as to what kind of spirituality is meant. *"He has not backed off what critics call creeping New Ageism. It's so close to what he's about,"* says mentor John Seigenthaler, *"It's his challenge TO THE SPIRITUAL LIFE OF THE NATION."*

CLINTON'S RELIGIOUS FAITH

Mr. Clinton talked about his religious faith in the July 20, 1992 *US News and World Report*, saying that he believed in a lot of old-fashioned things like the constancy of sin and the "possibility of forgiveness." One of the basic Baptist tenets, is the *absolute certainty* of forgiveness, when one accepts Jesus Christ as Savior - *NOT THE POSSIBILITY.*

He went on to say, *"I believe it in a Baptist way - that a lot of a person's spiritual journey should be intensely private and shared only with God."* This is again foreign to Baptist theology and heritage. Baptists are renown for making their faith and "spiritual journey" a public testimony. Baptists draw a great deal of comfort in the fact that, even in times of trial and trouble, they are exhorted to *"Bear ye one another's burdens, and so fulfill the law of Christ"* (Gal. 6:2). They are exhorted to comfort one another because they feel that they draw strength from the sharing of their faith.

The Great Commission, according to the Baptist Church is to take the gospel, the faith, to every kindred, nation and tongue. One of the hallmarks of the Baptist Church is it's zeal in sharing the faith. Baptists proudly attest that the very cornerstone of the Christian faith, is to make disciples of all nations. Their supporting text is found in Matthew 28:19-20, *"Go ye therefore, and teach all nations, baptizing them in the name of the Father, and of the Son, and of the Holy Ghost: Teaching them to*

*observe all things whatsoever I have commanded you:
and, lo, I am with you always, even unto the end of the
world. Amen."*

CHAPTER THREE

AL GORE'S VIEW OF
NEO-PAGAN FUNDAMENTALIST
RELIGIONS

In *Earth in the Balance: Ecology and the Human Spirit*, Al Gore, on pages 248-259, shows us just where he "departed" from the Baptist faith and entered the New Age. He attempts to diagnose the root problem of our Western culture:

"The richness and diversity of our religious tradition throughout history is a spiritual resource long *ignored by people of faith, who are often AFRAID TO OPEN THEIR MINDS to teachings FIRST OFFERED OUTSIDE THEIR OWN SYSTEM OF BELIEF*...This panreligious perspective may prove especially important where our global civilization's responsibility for the earth is concerned.

Native American Religions [witch doctors] - for instance, *offer a rich tapestry of ideas about our relationship to the earth. ONE OF THE MOST MOVING*...was attributed to Chief Seattle in 1855...

"..Will you teach your children what we have taught our children? THAT THE EARTH IS OUR MOTHER? What befalls the earth befalls all the sons of the earth. This we know: THE EARTH DOES NOT BELONG TO MAN, MAN BELONGS TO THE EARTH. All things are connected like the blood that unites us all.'"* (emphasis ours)

Gore continues with a string of illustrations that point readers to a pantheistic path that supposedly will restore our *"lost connection"* to the earth. For Example, "A modern prayer of the Onondaga tribe in upstate New York offers another beautiful expression of our essential connection to the earth: 'O Great Spirit, whose breath gives life to the world and whose voice is heard in the soft breeze. . .make us wise so that we may understand what you have taught us. . .'" (p. 259)

Ancient goddess worship fits right into this pantheistic panorama. It also seems to affirm Al Gore's own spiritual searchings and personal persuasions. After all, his view of today's environmental disasters demands both human intervention and spiritual empowerment - exactly what feminist and goddess spirituality offer. While Gore occasionally cloaks his arguments in Christian phrases, his overall plan calls for a "spiritual revival" that trades the Biblical God for a medley of spiritual substitutes.

Do you remember the distinction we made earlier between Baptist theology and New Age theology? Gore now believes that man has become one with the earth. As *Gore commends "the wisdom distilled by all faiths,"* he points to ancient goddess spirituality and Native American religions as models for finding "the spiritual sense of our place in nature."

When *Gore embraces "all faiths,"* he not only departs from Baptist theology, but from the Bible and from the faith it represents. God continually warned the Israelites not to become involved with pagans, or their beliefs and practices. In fact, the tendency on the part of the Israelites to attempt to "blend" the two brought severe judgment from the God of the Bible.

Seattle Fiasco

Who was Chief Seattle? How reliable is the information that Gore quotes and describes as *"one of the most moving?"* The words that touched Gore's heart so profoundly were not spoken by Chief Seattle. They were actually penned by Ted Perry for a 1971 environmental movie.

As we read the following sad account, we would hope that Gore's research on our behalf in the U.S. Senate is more thorough than his research on Chief Seattle. When a leader is placed into power, the people who place him there are "depending" upon his "accuracy" in representing them, and the issues that affect them.

According to the April 21, 1992 issue of the *New York Times,* "'Chief Seattle is probably our greatest manufactured prophet,' said David Buerge, a Northwest historian who is writing a book on the chief. He is one of the group of scholars frustrated that their work has failed to stop the myth from spreading around the world.

"An embellished version of a single speech given by the 68-year -old chief in 1854 makes him out to be an environmental prophet. *'The earth is our mother,'* says one version of the "letter" to Pierce. It goes on to say, "I have seen a thousand rotting buffaloes on the prairies left by the white man who shot them from a passing train.'

"But there were no bison within 500 miles of Seattle's home on Puget Sound; what's more, the letter is dated about 15 years before the first railroad crossed the Plains from Omaha to Sacramento, California. The great buffalo slaughter took place at least a decade after Seattle died.

"Will you teach your children what we have taught our children? That the earth is our mother? . . .This we know: the earth does not belong to man, man belongs to the earth. ALL THINGS ARE CONNECTED *like the blood that unites us all* (emphasis ours)."

Is Al Gore Promoting Pantheism?

Al Gore starts out in his book, on the very first page, by *immediately asserting his pantheistic beliefs,* "...we feel increasingly distant from our roots in the earth...civilization itself has been on a journey from its foundations in the world of nature to an ever more contrived, controlled, and manufactured world of our own imitative and sometimes arrogant design...At some point during this journey we lost our feeling of CONNECTEDNESS to the rest of nature...Are we so unique and powerful as to be essentially separate from the earth?...this perspective cannot treat the earth as something separate from human civilization; we are part of the whole too, and looking at it ultimately means also looking at ourselves...we seem to share a restlessness of spirit that rises out of the *LOST CONNECTION* to our world and our future."(emphasis ours)

You will note the repetition of the theme of "connectedness" throughout Gore's writings. He places great emphasis upon the importance of restoring our "connectedness" - as if we had, at one time, been attached by an invisible umbilical cord to Mother Earth. He leads us to believe that our whole world will soon crumble if we do not locate the "lost chord" and become reconnected to "our mother" the Earth.

ARE WE CONNECTED TO THE EARTH? IS THE EARTH OUR MOTHER?

While Mother Earth spirituality may sound foreign and remote to some, it is fast gaining a foothold in our nation. When people trade absolute truth and objective observation for personal persuasions and subjective opinions, they will believe anything. Suddenly the beliefs and practices of pagan religions are flooding our nation, invading school classrooms, and infiltrating our media.

Richard Ostling, in *Time Magazine*, May, 1991 told about one of the more overt pagan expressions of our changing culture,

"To mark Earth Day, four women and two men stood on a hilltop outside Mt. Horeb, Wisconsin, literally *praying to Mother Earth*. 'Sacred Earth Power, bring healing to Planet Earth,' intoned barefoot Selena Fox, priestess of Circle Sanctuary...Similar nature worship was part of Earth Day festivals from Boston...to Berkeley...The ceremonies were part of a growing U.S. spiritual movement: Goddess worship, the effort to create a *FEMALE-CENTERED* focus for spiritual expression.'" (emphasis ours)

Notice how they have now progressed from simply referring to *"Mother Earth,"* to bestowing divinity upon her as a *"goddess,"* and *actually praying to and worshiping the "goddess."*

New Age writer Elinor Gadon, wrote in *The Once and Future Goddess*, "In the late twentieth century there is a growing awareness that we are doomed as a species and planet unless we have a *RADICAL CHANGE OF CONSCIOUSNESS. The reemergence of the GODDESS is becoming the SYMBOL AND METAPHOR for this TRANSFORMATION*...[and] has led to a new earth-based spirituality." (emphasis ours)

From the Christian viewpoint, how does God view all of this: Isaiah 42:5,8 *"Thus saith the Lord God, he that created the heavens, and stretched them out; he that spread forth the earth, and that which comes out of it;*

he that gives breath unto the people upon it, and spirit to them that walk therein...I am the Lord: that is my name: and my glory will I not give to another, neither my praise to graven images."

THE NEW COVENANT OF BILL CLINTON AND AL GORE

CHAPTER FOUR

AL GORE AND HIS SPIRITUAL NEW AGE AGENDA

Al Gore's book, *Earth in the Balance: Ecology and the Human Spirit* that is taking the nation by storm, provides us with a vast wealth of shocking information. His actual writings will make it easier for us to ascertain what he really believes. They also raise a valid question to consider as we ponder his strange philosophy. As vice president of the USA, would he attempt to force-feed it to the American people under the guise of wise environmentalism?

On pages 238-239, he states, "Whether we believe that our dominion derives from God or from our own ambition, there is little doubt that the way we currently relate to the environment is wildly inappropriate. But in order to change, we have to address some fundamental questions about our purpose in life, our capacity to direct the *POWERFUL INNER FORCES* that have created this crisis, and who we are. These questions go beyond any discussion of whether the human species is an appropriate technology; *THESE QUESTIONS ARE NOT FOR*

THE MIND OR THE BODY BUT THE SPIRIT."
(emphasis ours)

Pantheism: Religion of the New Age

The *CONNECTEDNESS* Gore invisions flows through the core of the world's pantheistic religions. Pantheism, as defined in Webster's New World Dictionary, *"...is the belief that God is not a personality, but that all forces, manifestations, etc. of the universe are God...the worship of all gods."* In other words, pantheists view God as an impersonal force that is in all parts of nature, making everything sacred and joining all things together as one spiritually connected entity (monism).

Does Al Gore make the distinction between fundamental neo-pagan pantheism and Biblical Christianity? On pages 264-265 he clearly makes the distinction between the two,

"We are not used to seeing God in the world because we assume from the scientific and philosophical rules that govern us that the physical world is made up of inanimate matter whirling in accordance with mathematical laws and bearing no relation to life, much less ourselves. *WHY DOES IT FEEL FAINTLY HERETICAL TO A CHRISTIAN TO SUPPOSE THAT GOD IS IN US AS HUMAN BEINGS?..IT IS MY OWN BELIEF THAT THE IMAGE OF GOD CAN BE SEEN IN EVERY CORNER OF CREATION, EVEN IN US.*"

New Environmentalism and Goddess Worship

Al Gore reveals his own personal relationship with this new environmentalism of the spirit. On page 242 of his book he states, "...it may now be necessary to foster a new "environmentalism of the spirit." Spirit! What spirit? He provides us with the answer to this question in his book!

On page 260, Al Gore clearly reveals his own understanding concerning Goddess Worship. He states, "The *spiritual* sense of OUR place in nature predates Native American cultures...A growing number of anthropologists and archaeo-*mythologists,* such as Marija Gimbutas and Rian Eisler, argue that the prevailing ideology of belief in prehistoric Europe and much of the world was based on the worship of *A SINGLE EARTH GODDESS*, who was assumed to be the fount of all life and who radiated harmony among all living things...the evidence for the existence of this primitive *RELIGION* comes from the many 1000's of artifacts uncovered in ceremonial sites. *THESE SITES ARE SO WIDESPREAD THAT THEY SEEM TO CONFIRM THE NOTION THAT A GODDESS RELIGION WAS U-BIQUITOUS* throughout much of the world *UNTIL the antecedents of TODAY'S religions - most of which still have a DISTINCTLY MASCULINE ORIENTATION -* almost obliterating belief in the goddess. *The last vestige of ORGANIZED GODDESS WORSHIP WAS ELIMINATED BY CHRISTIANITY* as late as the 15th century in Lithuania...the archaeological scholarship is impressive, and *it seems obvious THAT A BETTER UNDER-STANDING OF A RELIGIOUS HERITAGE PRE-CEDING OUR OWN BY SO MANY 1000's OF YEARS COULD OFFER US NEW INSIGHTS* into the nature of the human experience.

On page 261, Gore cites yet another neo-pagan (the contemporary form of ancient paganism) source of wisdom for today's environmental crisis: "One modern Hindu environmentalist, Dr. Karan Singh, regularly cites the ancient Hindu dictum: *'THE EARTH IS OUR MOTHER, AND WE ARE ALL HER CHILDREN.'*

Al Gore and Bible Prophecy Students

Al Gore seems to have words of praise for all the neo-pagan religions of the world, but only disdain for those who truly belong to "His Faith"- i.e., Baptists who control the Southern Baptist Convention. Mr. Gore, in referring to Bible believing Christians, says on page 263, "F*or some Christians, (Bible believers) the prophetic vision of the apocalypse is used - IN MY VIEW, UN-FORGIVABLY* -[his version of *the UNPARDONABLE SIN?]*.

CHAPTER FIVE

CLINTON AND GORE - DYNAMIC DUO OF THE POLITICALLY CORRECT

A New Face for "Big Brother"

As we face what could be one of the most critical elections in modern history, we MUST become well-informed. This book is definitely not a partisan treatise, because the Republican candidates have problems too. What you and I must be concerned with, however, is the protection of freedoms, especially our religious freedom, that could vanish as quickly as the morning dew.

Heretofore, political campaigns conducted by the Democratic Party were just that - political. But suddenly, we see a drastic change - the introduction of the "spiritual," by those who have cried loudest that we must maintain "separation of church and state."

Why this drastic change in terminology and strategy? Why would a presidential nominee who is the vital link of the liberal left suddenly "appear" to swing from left to just right of center?

The headlines and succeeding story in the July 13, 1992 issue of *USA Today* reveal this closely thought out strategy. The headline reads, "Election '92 Democrats pull out all the stops." The article is headed, "Tired of losing elections," and it spells out the new campaign plan. "After losing five of the past six presidential elections, Democrats open their 1992 convention here today thinking they've finally figured out how to win.

"They will try to showcase the party as a mirror image of mainstream America, not a loose collection of angry liberals with a potpourri of pet peeves to air, or old political scores to settle.

"In a sense, they've copied the Republican playbook and crafted a tightly scripted, God-family-and-apple-pie convention aimed at convincing angry voters that the Democratic Party is one of them."

HOW MUCH DID GORE'S NEW AGE BELIEFS HAVE TO DO WITH HIS SELECTION AS THE VICE-PRESIDENTIAL NOMINEE?

Tom Cronin, a well-known political scientist at Colorado College, predicted Gore would be a popular choice because he "...does what is right," for political reasons. In other words, he's PC.

Mr. Cronin was so impressed with Gores' New Age book that he stated, *"I never remember reading a book by a public official that has so much impact,"* so much so that he bought a copy for his son.

It is common knowledge that no one can reach the political heights Bill Clinton and Al Gore have without being " PC" or "politically correct."

To be politically correct is to be in conformity with the global environmental thinkers who are moving this country and the world into the one world political-economic and religious system the Bible predicted would come.

The Media - From Objectivity to Advocacy

In fact, if someone, or some thing, becomes PC, then even *the media, who are supposed to be totally objective, become suddenly "subjective."*

According to the October 20, 1989 issue of *The Wall Street Journal*, "Charles Alexander declared, 'As the science editor at Time *I would freely admit that on this [environmental] issue we have crossed the boundary from news reporting to advocacy.'* After a round of applause from the gathered journalists and scientists, *NBC correspondent Andrea Mitchell told the audience that 'clearly the networks have made that decision* now, where you'd have to call it advocacy.' (emphasis ours)

"At that point, *Washington Post editor Benjamin Bradlee chimed in, saying 'I don't think there's any danger in doing what you suggest.* There's a rumor danger in saying it because as soon as you say, *"To hell with the news, I'm no longer interested in news, I'm interested in causes*, you've got a WHOLE KOOKY CONSTITUENCY to respond to which you CAN WASTE A LOT OF TIME ON." (emphasis ours)

"Mr. Bradlee is right. Probably a lot of "kooks" believe in objective journalism. . . .

"Somehow the idea has gotten around that the environment isn't a normal political issue, but a quasi-religious crusade. As a result, public discussion of the environment has been about as rigorous as one expects from a jihad."

David Brooks, the author of this article is exactly right. It is a jihad, "holy war," and who has made it that? Politicians like Al Gore who infuse the "spiritual" aspect into what could have been a scientific issue.

Brooks goes on to say, "The shortcomings of advocacy were very much in evidence at the recent environmental conference sponsored by the Smithsonian Institution. Held in the original museum buildings that celebrate the achievements of the Industrial Revolution, the meeting addressed the topic, "The Global Environment: Are We Overreacting?" *Every other time I have been to a conference organized around a question, there have been speakers on both sides. But not this time.*

*Through the entire conference, not a single disagree-
ment deflected the steady breeze of alarmism.*

"Perpetual apocalyptics such as Lester Brown and Paul
Ehrlich rattled off their anthems of doom. . . .Speakers
and panels moved briskly on and off the podium: acid
rain crisis, a famine crisis, a population crisis. The result
was a smorgasbord of apocalypse.

"On the subject of global warming, a frisky environmental policy analyst named Stephen H. Schneider,
presented the gloom and doom side of the global warming debate. *A number of scientists are more skeptical
about global warming, such as Hugh W. Ellsaesser of
the Livermore National Library, Reid Bryson of the
University of Wisconsin, Richard Lindzen of MIT, V.
Ramathan of the University of Chicago and Andrew
Solow of the Woods Hole Institute of Oceanography.
But they were not to be heard from.*

"The same sort of stage-managing prevailed among
journalist speakers. Barbara Pyle, who is the head of
Turner Broadcasting Network's International Documen-
tary Unit. . .'internationally recognized environmental
activist,' appeared on a panel. *Many reporters do not
see the rules of objective journalism as obstacles to
social progress. But they were not to be heard from.*

"*The conference was co-chaired by the CEOs of ABC,
NBC, CBS, Turner Broadcasting Network, Time
Warner and the Los Angeles Times, the director of the
New York Times and senior officers of other media*

institutions. Dow Jones wasn't involved. Apparently none of these journalistic companies insisted upon diversity of opinion.

"Thomas Lovejoy [one of Gore's key advisors in his book]. . .eloquently encouraged the idea that we are in a planetary crisis. 'The planet is about to break out with fever and indeed it may have already,' he said, "and we are the disease.'

". . .Mr. Lovejoy suggested that 'we should be at war with ourselves and with our life styles.' The anti-growth contingent also made its presence felt. Mr. Erlich declared, "WE'VE ALREADY HAD TOO MUCH ECONOMIC GROWTH IN THE UNITED STATES. . . ECONOMIC GROWTH IN RICH COUNTRIES LIKE OURS IS THE DISEASE, NOT THE CURE."

CHAPTER SIX

THE NEW COVENANT AND "TRADITIONAL FAMILY VALUES"

Democratic Presidential and Vice-Presidential nominees Bill Clinton and Al Gore have outlined *"A New Covenant"* where *"family and traditional values"* will be focused upon by this new team. This is strange coming from two men who champion the killing of the unborn, unnatural homosexual lifestyles, and a myriad of values that are certainly not "traditional."

The idea of "traditional values" in the Democratic Party is something that is rather strange. Its association with liberal left-wing causes has always put it at odds with "traditional values" as we have known them.

Marriage = Slavery

Hillary Clinton likens marriage to slavery, according to an article in *Human Events*, July 11, 1992. "Writing in a 1982 issue of the Harvard Educational Review, Hillary

Clinton likened the American family to "marriage, slavery, and the Indian reservation." The Clinton quote was turned up by Daniel Wattenberg of the Washington Times.

"Wattenberg also discovered that Hillary Clinton filed her 1991 tax returns under her own name of Hillary Rodham which she used until her husband entered the presidential race.

"Hillary Rodham Clinton also reported a capital gain from De Beer's, the South African diamond company, at the height of apartheid."

"'Women' creator to push political agenda" is the title of an article appearing in *Christians and Society Today* magazine: "Producer Linda Bloodworth-Thomason - who took off on the Clarence Thomas hearings last season on CBS' *Designing Women* - says she'll push the boundaries even further this fall.

"*Bloodworth-Thomason, who is helping Gov. Bill Clinton's presidential campaign, said she initially worried that "equal time" requirements might keep her from discussing politics on Designing Women this fall. But the Federal Communications Commission said she can say whatever, as long as candidates don't appear.*"

Baptists and Moral Breakdown

"Baptists decry society's moral breakdown." *The Christians and Society Today* magazine also carried this article from *The Clarion Ledger,* June 12, 1992. "Southern Baptists, blasting what they called 'the moral breakdown in our society,' accused television networks of promoting immorality and demanded that public schools quit giving out condoms.

"The Baptists, in the final day of their three-day annual convention, also encouraged Boy Scouts of America to continue to ban homosexuals from leadership positions and to retain the pledge of duty to God in the Scout oath.

"Delegates to the 15.2 million-member denomination's convention also passed resolutions AGAINST SUICIDE, ABORTION AND ABORTION- RELATED RESEARCH. . . (emphasis ours)

"In a resolution condemning the distribution of condoms in public schools, the delegates expressed "moral outrage at this unprecedented usurpation of parental rights and violation of family integrity."

Speaking of the Southern Baptist Convention, and we know that both Clinton and Gore claim to be Baptists - why were they not invited to speak instead of Dan Quayle, a Presbyterian. Are the Southern Baptists so terribly inconsiderate at such a crucial time in history -

57

or is there a definite "difference" in the way they define Baptist and the definitions of Gore and Clinton?

Family values...Baptist...Abortion...Public Schools full of integrity. . .Anti-Private Schools and Home Schooling. . .Marriage = Slavery?

We hear the words, but somehow they just do not ring true to our ears, that is unless there is a new English grammar rule that make antonyms and synonyms the same.

Dysfunctional Families - The Worst is Yet to Come

Gore also has some interesting ideas on families. In his book, *he describes a "dysfunctional family." On page 226* we read, "The idea of the dysfunctional family was first developed by theorists such as R.D. Laing, Virginia Satir, Gregory Bateson, Milton Erickson, Murray Bowen, Nathan Ackerman, and Alice Miller, and more recently it has been refined and brought to a popular audience by writers like John Bradshaw. *The problem they have all sought to explain is how families made up of well-meaning, seemingly normal individuals can engender destructive relationships among themselves,* driving individual family members as well as their family system into crisis.

"According to the theory of dysfunctionality, unwritten rules governing how to raise children and purporting to determine what it means to be a human being are passed down from one generation of a family to the next. The modern version of these rules was shaped by the same philosophical world view that led to the scientific and technological revolution: it defines human beings as primarily intellectual entities detached from the physical world. [not an integral part of nature]. . . .

Patriarchal vs Matriarchal - Who's the Boss?

"One consequence of this scientific view was a changed understanding of God. Once it became clear that science - instead of divine provenance - might explain many of nature's mysteries, it seemed safe to assume that the creator, having set the natural world in motion within discernible and predictable patterns, was somewhat removed and detached from the world, out there above us looking down. Families came to be seen as Ptolemaic systems, with the *FATHER AS THE PA-TRIARCH AND SOURCE OF AUTHORITY* and all the other family members orbiting around him. This change had a dramatic effect on children. Before the scientific era, children almost certainly found it easier to locate and understand their place in the world because they could define themselves in relation both to their parents and to A GOD WHO WAS CLEARLY PRE-SENT IN NATURE." (emphasis ours)

The time he is describing predating the "patriarchal" family is the era of pantheism - which believed that God was in every part of nature and that nature was God.

Thus they worshiped the Sun, the Moon, Constellations and every aspect of nature - rather than the Creator of nature - God.

"With these two firm points of reference, children were less likely to lose their direction in life. But with God receding from the natural world to an abstract place, [*Baptists do not believe their heart is an abstract place, nor that God is removed from them into the distant heavens, but alive and dwelling in their spirits at every moment - present tense.*] *THE PATRIARCHAL FIGURE IN THE FAMILY (ALMOST ALWAYS THE FATHER)* effectively became God's viceroy, *entitled to exercise godlike authority when enforcing family rules. . . .children became confused* about their own roles in a family system that was *severely stressed by the demands of the DOMINANT, ALL-POWERFUL FATHER.* (emphasis ours)

Gore says he believes in traditional family values, but what we see emerging from his writings is someone who is unsure of his own role in the family. He attaches so much emphasis on the "matriarchal" role, that we wonder if he even knows what the definition of a "traditional family" is - according to most Americans. Gore, as his fellow Democratic National Committee staffer so avidly points out, seems as if he feels "guilty" about his own role as a man. He is so confused, so weak-kneed and so out of tune with mainstream America, how could we possibly have any degree of confidence in his leadership?

"Parents were accorded godlike authority to enforce the rules, and, as Bradshaw and others argue, one of the most basic rules that emerged is that the rules themselves cannot be questioned. . . .one of the ways our civilization secures adherence to its rules is by teaching the separation of people from the natural world and suppressing the emotions that might allow us to feel the absence of OUR CONNECTION TO THE EARTH."

These are not the "Family Values" of the Bible. It is plain that the God and family relationships described in the Holy Scriptures are TOTALLY FOREIGN to Gore. *Gore, by his own statements describes his view of a distant God, and the repulsiveness of His authority.* He does not describe the gentle, personal, loving, ever-present God of Baptists or Christians in general.

Al Gore's Mentors

If he does not get his views from the Bible, from whom did he get his social philosophy? Virginia Satir is one of those. In her book, *Meditations and Inspirations*, she writes, "Recognize that we all come from the same life-force, *equipped with the potential for helping ourselves to become fully evolved.* . . .Be aware that you have energy to use for yourself. *This energy comes from the center of the earth*, it moves through your feet and legs and grounds you. . . .

"Now say to yourself, 'I am able, I can do this. *I have the energy through my groundedness*, my relationship

61

to the heavens and my interconnectedness with others. I am able'" (emphasis ours)

Virginia Satir, according to Berit Kjos, author of *Under the Spell of Mother Earth*, is a "family therapist and founder of Avanta Network, an international organization dedicated to developing techniques for teaching family and professional communication. "Satir, whose books have found amazing acceptance among educators, has developed her own blend of empowering imagery, Eastern pantheism, and Goddess spirituality:

'Dreams and wishes can be manifested. Use the power of a golden wishing wand to make it happen. Picture your golden wishing wand in your hand. Endow that wand with the ability to remove your fear of risk-taking. . . .Feel the texture, look at the form. It's yours, for the rest of your life, to use in whatever way you want.'

"In *Meditations and Inspirations*, she guides her students into a dreamy state of consciousness where they build their own psychic workshop and redesign their lives. How? *Through centering* [Remember, Gore speaks of how he became "centered."], *deep breathing, affirmations, focusing, visualizations - the magical formulas of earth-centered spirituality.* 'I own me,' she writes, speaking for the multitude of school children, educators, church leaders, and modern therapists who love her books and teach her message. 'Therefore, I can engineer me.'

"The creator counters the lie with truth: 'You are not your own; you were bought with a price.' (I Corinthians 6:19)" (*Under the Spell of Mother Earth*, Berit Kjos)

Gore also espouses the teachings of John Bradshaw. Let's see what this guru to Christians, as well as New Agers [Bradshaw] advocates: "There is also evidence that this consciousness is connected to all created consciousness. The early work of J. B. Rhine at Duke in telepathy pointed clearly in this direction. The more recent work of Putoff and Targ at Stanford Research Institute (SRI) on Remote Viewing E.S.P. has offered powerful new data suggesting that once in higher consciousness, we have a higher power available to us. Their belief is that this power results from being *CON-NECTED* (emphasis ours) to all other created consciousness.

"There are also ancient traditions supporting a higher power through expanded consciousness. The Indian Medicine Healers believed there was a greater power available through the use of meditation and the fusion with power animals. *Jesus told His followers that there were powers available to them that were greater than the powers He manifested. His human powers were clearly powers of psychokinesis, clairvoyance, telepathy and precognition.*"

Gore again refers to Bradshaw on page 227, ". . .one of the ways our civilization secures adherence to its rules is by teaching the separation of people from the natural world and suppressing the emotions that might allow us to feel the absence of our *CONNECTION TO THE EARTH*." (emphasis ours)

Bradshaw speaks of the *CONNECTEDNESS* (emphasis ours) which seems to be an important theme to Gore since it is woven through his book with great emphasis.

Bradshaw is also a proponent of Abraham Maslow's theory of *self-actualization*, even though Maslow saw its dangers before he died and tried to correct the damages. Self-actualization is the theory that our central purpose and goal in life is to fulfill "the self." It teaches that the greater part of our energies should be focused on fully developing "self" and fulfilling, to the uttermost, all "self's" desires and ambitions. *Maslow later found that when children were taught self-actualization, they broke loose from the safety of parental boundaries, and became unteachable and unruly.*

We see the same attitudes now evidenced in the products of the public school system. As children are taught that they have control over their own lives and destinies, that they should be free to make their own choices and decisions, they fall into every trap the devil sets to ensnare them. To further complicate the matter, the school teaches them that if parents attempt to discipline them, that their rights have been violated, and they can report their parents for "abuse." Therefore, *in the public school system and in the system of Al Gore,* there are no absolutes - except that a parent now has lost the right to raise his own child according to Biblical principles.

Gore goes on to quote Ashley Montagu on page 229, ". . .As Ashley Montagu first pointed out decades ago, *evolution encouraged the development of larger and larger human brains, but our origins in the primate family* [diametrically opposed to the Baptist doctrine of Creation] placed a limit on the ability of the birth canal to accommodate babies with ever-larger heads. Nature's solution was to encourage an extremely long period of dependence on the nurturing parent during infancy and childhood, allowing both mind and body to continue developing in an almost gestational way long after birth. But as a result of this long period of social and psychological development, children are extremely vulnerable to both good and bad influences, and in a dysfunctional family, that means they will absorb and integrate the dysfunctional rules and warped assumptions about life that are being transmitted by the parents."

Friend, do you remember who Gore said was responsible for dysfunctional families? **The patriarchal system of Christianity!**

According to an article, entitled **"Idyllic Theory of Goddess Creates Storm,"** by Peter Steinfels, *New York Times*, February 13, 1990, Ashley Montague (*whom Gore just quoted*), hailed the book, *The Language of the Goddess,* by Marija Gimbutas as "a benchmark in the history of civilization." Let's see what Marija wrote that is so wonderful: "Long ago, explains Dr. Gimbutas, *when matriarchal societies worshiped Goddesses, people lived in harmony with one another and with nature.* Queen-priestesses ruled clans and shunned war. But, somewhere, around 4000 B.C., *patriarchal invaders deposed the life-giving Goddess and shattered the original peace and equality. . .*

"*Forced underground, the Goddess religion maintained a cultural foothold through Greek and Roman female deities, the Virgin Mary, and cultural myths, symbols. . . .Through centuries, 'a substratum of Old Europe survived in harvest customs and peasant beliefs about springs, rocks, trees, and animals, in medieval magic* and THE PRACTICES THAT CHRISTIAN AUTHORITIES PERSECUTED AS WITCH-CRAFT.'* (Idyllic Theory of Goddess Creates Storm, *New York Times*, 2/13/90)" (*Under the Spell of Mother Earth*, Berit Kjos)

THESE ARE QUOTES FROM THE PEOPLE GORE CONSIDERS AS TRUE AND CREDIBLE. If they have shocked you, as they did me, I cannot add adequate words to convey my horror at the conclusion we both must draw. You see, *you and I are a part of the "ENEMY" called PATRIARCHAL CHRISTIANITY which seems to draw the utmost contempt from our Vice Presidential candidate - God help us all!*

CHAPTER SEVEN

PC "POLITICALLY CORRECT" IN EDUCATION

New Age Child Sacrifice

What is the best and most effective way to gain total control of a nation or society? Through the "youth" of course. The communists were aware of this and developed political brainwashing clubs, like "Young Pioneers," to gain the allegiance and devotion of the youth. You see, us older folk are already "set" in our ways and belief systems, while young minds are like a new chalkboard, ready to be written on - to be programmed.

The noted humanist advocate, John Dunphy wrote, *"I am convinced that the battle for humankind's future must be waged and won in the public school classroom by teachers. . . .These teachers must embody the same selfless dedication as the most rabid fundamentalist preachers, for they will be ministers of another sort, utilizing a classroom instead of a pulpit to convey humanist values in whatever subject they teach, regardless of the educational level - preschool, day-care or large state university.*

"The classroom must and will become the arena of conflict between the old and the new - THE ROTTING CORPSE OF CHRISTIANITY, together with all its adjacent evils and misery, and the new faith of humanism. Humanism will emerge triumphant. It must if the family of humankind is to survive."

Jobe Martin, featured author in *The Bulletin*, August, 1992 describes techniques introduced into the public school system to break down family ties, **"Duso the Dolphin is a puppet who also asks children to discuss personal problems in class.** *DUSO I,* for kindergarten and first grade children, *employs relaxation and breathing techniques and uses guided fantasies to hypnotize youngsters.*

"DUSO is clearly founded on humanistic precepts with methods and materials that target the child's fixed beliefs. **God, of course, is nonexistent in the world of DUSO.**

"Impressions, which is designed to teach language arts, has dark lessons that are repeated and amplified in the children's project books. . . .In this series, **FIRST THROUGH SIXTH GRADERS WILL BE TAUGHT HOW TO CAST SPELLS AND WILL BE ASKED WHICH HORRIBLE DEATH THEY WOULD PREFER.**

"Whatever the particular subject matter, *these programs follow standard brainwashing techniques of putting the victims under emotional stress, breaking down their inhibitions and destroying their links to others on the outside.*

"With school children, the link that must be loosened or broken is the child's link to his or her parents. In innumerable ways, some very subtle, these programs undermine or ridicule parents. *Sometimes children are explicitly told not to tell anyone, including their parents, what is said in the "magic circle," a typical term for these classroom brainwashing sessions."*

Change Agents in the Schools

If you think this sounds bizzare, believe it or not, teachers and students are currently being tested to determine their "beliefs," and "values." We now have *"change agents" in our public school system* whose job it is to correct those beliefs that do not align with the one-world agenda of the Politically Correct.

Most parents are totally unaware of what is going on - the reshaping of our children's minds! An article that appeared in the January 20, 1992 *Tulsa World*, on the front page of the Sunday edition may shed some light on how secretive and clandestine *"Change Agents" are at work in our public schools.*

The article is entitled, "Air of Secrecy Surrounds Tests," serves to illustrate how far Big Brother is reaching into the minds of our children to gain control of their behavior. The article stated that 100 Oklahoma school *children were taking federally sponsored tests which opponents say are aimed at identifying and CHANGING students' values and beliefs.* Incredibly, the state school superintendent and state testing director both said they knew nothing about the tests, except that they were given directly to local schools by the U.S. Department of Education.

These tests appear to be so controversial that federal officials refused to disclose where the tests were given and that it would be more than a year before they would release copies of the test to the press.

According to Steve Gorman, a U.S. Department of Education project officer, *"The law requires that they be confidential.* It's not a secret. It's to keep the pressure off and keep the press out of the school." *If it is not secret, why won't they let the parents whose children have taken these tests look at them?* Anita Hoge, a Pennsylvania mother who led a fight against VALUES TESTING in that state said, "They have a criteria of HOW they want a child to RESPOND to a social event. They're not graded by grammar, punctuation, spelling or composition."

Perhaps all of this emphasis by the U.S. Department of Education to develop children for the New World Order by imposing social, multi-cultural and behavioral modification techniques, is responsible for the horrible academic rating of American students as compared with other nations.

According to *USA Today*, February 6, 1992, *"U.S. Students once again, have scored near the bottom in the most comprehensive test ever to compare their math and science skills with those in other countries.* Education Secretary Lamar Alexander said, "This is not the kind of report that an American who likes to be first should be happy about."

In science, the U.S. students tested finished ahead of ONLY IRELAND AND JORDAN among 15 countries. In math, U.S. students were SECOND FROM THE BOTTOM.

Despite our horrible academic showing, and pressure from concerned parents about what is really being taught to our students, *the "tests" still remain a closely guarded SECRET. National Assessment of Education Progress spokesperson Tong Soo Song said that the test is exempt from the FREEDOM OF INFORMATION ACT* which is designed to give the public access to government records.

According to B.K. Eakman, author of *Educating for the New World Order*, the exams include questions aimed at assessing what children believe about social and emotional issues. *If we examine the picture of "The A+ Decision-Making and Management System for A+Achieving Excellence," we see in the "Implementa-*

tion" section, under "Tactics," the number one goal is to "Change beliefs." Results of tests are used to evaluate a community's beliefs and SELECT A CURRICU- LUM THAT WILL ALTER OR CORRECT ANY BELIEF OR VALUE that does not fit in with their idea of a New World Order.

The State of Illinois believes that only the PC are qualified to teach English. A competency test required of teachers in the state is almost completely a PC test. It requires that teachers deal with 15 passages written "by largely unknown feminists, Black, Asian, S. American, Indian or African authors."

The authors not included - Shakespeare, Melville, Dickens, Tennyson or Milton. Is it any wonder why U.S. students only rank ahead of 2 countries when the last international tests were conducted?

Clinton-NEA Love-In

Bill Clinton wants to take away your right to educate your child according to "your own" beliefs and val- ues. Bill Clinton also wants to force you to continue to pay the "bill" to educate other people's children in a system that is diametrically opposed to everything you believe. At the same time, Bill Clinton vehemently speaks out to deny you funds to educate your own children as you choose.

As recently as the week of July 12-18, Mr. Clinton reassured the public school teachers of the National Education Association that *"we shouldn't give our money away to private schools* (he's referring to our right to send our children to Christian schools or home school them) in *a way that will undermine the integrity of the public school system."* Clinton is definitely not "pro- choice" in education.

Clinton is saying that Christian schools and home schooling are detrimental, or dangerous to the public school system, and that they should not get one penny! Must we shout again, "No taxation without representation!" Many tax dollars are being forcefully taken from dissenting individuals who believe the public school system is inadequate academically, not to mention a travesty of religious freedom. He claims to be a Baptist, but he had rather give his money, and force us to give ours, to have children educated in occult and satanic practices rather than the Bible.

He said this even though, in cities like Chicago, the public school system has dismally failed to educate the very poor - those Mr. Clinton claims to care most about. THIS IS HYPOCRISY AT IT'S WORST!

"OK, Then You Have to Die."

The Dallas Child: The Monthly Parenting Magazine, February 1992, carried the following horror story.

73

"Amber came home one day and said, 'Mom, my teacher told us today that we're all gods.' I was stunned.

"The pothole that detoured (this mother) into the homeschool road came when her daughter, as part of a self-reliance/decision-making exercise, was told to seek a 'wise person.'

"She was crying one afternoon and said she didn't know who her wise person was, says (the mother). I told her it was God. She said, 'But when we're in our circles, we're supposed to talk to our wise person inside us. I can't talk to God, Mommy. I can't pray in class.' A few days later Amber came home crying again. ' I died in school today,' she sobbed. 'We were in a plane crash and the teacher made us go from door to door to get out, and I couldn't find the door. She said to seek my wise person. I told her it was God and she said, 'OK, then, you have to die.'"

(emphasis ours)

Bill Clinton: **"We shouldn't give our money away to private schools (he's referring to our right to send our children to Christian schools or home school them) in a way that will undermine the integrity of the public school system."**

As president and vice president, will Al Gore and Bill Clinton - *the "Dynamic Duo" of the politically correct* embody everything we envision the "Big Brother" of George Orwell to be? Would Gore's pagan beliefs be reinforced by Clinton to fuel America's growing enchantment with the Gaia-Mother Earth-Goddess environmental movement?

Since this neo-pagan ideology has now become "politically correct," will it be forced upon Christians and upon their children by the state? The groundwork is already in place, it has already, unbeknown to most parents, been pushed into our public school system. Now all that is left to do is to legally eradicate the rights of Bible believing Christians to speak out against it.

EARTH CHILD - Pagan Religion in Our Schools

As I referred to the concept of the "Gaia-Mother Earth Goddess" in the previous paragraph, you may not even be aware of what I was talking about - but your children probably are. Nonsense, you say. Please take the time to examine, and keep examining what books are used in your local public schools. Following is an excerpt from a curriculum taken from a school resource textbook right here in Broken Arrow, Oklahoma, the buckle of the Bible Belt. If your school doesn't have this or similar curriculum yet, it will.

"The name 'Gaia' refers to the Greek goddess of Earth. As the story goes, Gaia, the Earth, came out of darkness so long ago that no one really remembers or knows when or how. She was young, and since nothing lived on her yet to keep her company, she was also very lonely. One solitary night Uranus, the Sky, rose above her. He was beautiful to behold, strewn with sparkling stars against his dark blue sky. Gaia looked up at him and immediately fell in love. They gazed upon each other and smiled, and soon they were joined in love. Young Earth then became Mother Earth, the Mother of all living things. . .

The ancient Greeks loved and respected their mother, the Earth. . .they praised her and made offerings to her, so that she would always care for them." (*Earth Child*, Sheehan and Waidner)

In this new public school resource tool called *"Earth Child," they recommend celebrating pagan festivals, and encourage the children to make offerings to pagan deities.* Some of the ceremonies include: "Fire Ceremony in Honor of the Sun," "Celebrate the Fall Moon," a "Cosmic Celebration," "Mother Earth Pageant," and the "Gaia Earth Festival Honoring Mother Earth."

Earth Child, is now being used in grades K-3, with ongoing application through grade 12. It attempts to make children aware of the earth's environment and ecological systems. In doing this, however, the authors delve into what is known as *"deep ecology"* where the problem faced by man are addressed in a religious manner employing Hindu and pantheistic religious philosophies and doctrines. Those who practice "deep ecology" do, indeed, treat it as a religion, and, have been known to go to what most people would refer to as "fanatical" extremes to save plants, animals, habitats, etc.

Earth Child contains many facets of the practice of "deep ecology" in the form of exercises and games to be played in the classroom, which are referred to as "ceremonies" or "rituals" and which contain definite religious overtones from the Hindu religion and other pantheistic theologies.

On page 63, *children are told to make "offerings" to and "set aside a day to honor our Mother, the Earth."* This is in connection with the story about Gaia, the Greek goddess of Earth.

Page 88 contains a "fire Ceremony in Honor of the Sun" which has children reciting "We are the children of the Sun," and an adult "reader" telling them "The sun is the basis of all life on Earth," and **"You are a child of the Sun."**

Page 154 refers to the trees as our brother or sisters, yet in the fire "ceremony," when putting a log on a fire, the children are told to say: "Energy from the sun has been stored in the fibers of this wood for hundreds of years. We are going to set it free." (As they burn their "brother" or "sister" tree).

On page 222, the book states, "Every part of this earth is sacred. Every shining needle, every sandy shore, every mist in the dark woods, every meadow, and every animal bird or humming insect is holy." You are part of the earth and it is part of you. The perfumed flowers are your sisters, the deer, the horse, the great eagle, these are your brothers. . .The earth does not belong to you; you belong to the earth."

Also, see page 59 for the "ritual" in the "ceremony" of the Feast of the First Flower.

This book also uses *guided imagery* and verbal cues in what it calls *"Dream Starter"* which includes *deep breathing, massage, and speaking in a "soft and rhythmic tone" much like hypnosis.* In addition, the Maypole, an occult symbol, is danced around by the children as told on page 61.

School Replaces Christmas with Satanic, Occult Celebration

Another example of the blatant violation of our religious freedom comes from Texe Marrs' *Flashpoint* newsletter, June 1992. In a Portland, Oregon elementary school, the children were told that they would not be allowed to celebrate Christmas this year because that would be wrong - Church and State must be kept separate. Right?

On December 19, 1991, in the place of the Christmas event, the children would, instead, be required to participate in a "Winter Solstice Program." This is historically, a witchcraft and satanic holiday in which occult astrology and chanting are employed with worship of the Sun God and Moon Goddess.

"The cover of the official printed program handed out to students and parents was revealing. It depicted *the Sun God (Lucifer, god of light) and the Moon Goddess* (see Rev. 17 - Mystery Babylon).

"Inside the printed program. . .is found this description of the Winter Solstice Program:

'Each child will partake of the sun and moon cake before entering the auditorium, where they will seat themselves *according to their astrological signs. . .Chanting will begin on entering the auditorium. . .*

'The Sun God and Moon Goddess will enter with attendants.'

"The cakes to be eaten are the same ones devoured by the heathen worshipers of the god Baal (Sun God) and the goddess Ashtoreth (the Moon Goddess) in the ritual denounced as an abomination by God in our Bible (see books of Ezekiel, Jeremiah, and I Kings).

". . .The Solstice program included New Age dancing and pagan drumming. A number of children came dressed-up as 'trees and animal spirits' (coyotes, hawks, frogs, etc.). Songs like This Little Light of Mine and Bye, Bye Blackbird were sung and birds were released to 'fly into the universe.'"

The Mark of the Beast Introduced in School

In one segment of the school's Solstice program, children came in with Bar Codes stamped on their foreheads. The Bar Codes of some were read and ACCEPTED, but others, WHO DID NOT HAVE THE PROPER MARK were REJECTED. Only those who had the CHOSEN MARK were deemed "good and worthy."

This pagan, anti-Christian hypocrisy is found in the New Age curriculum called, *"Pumsy in Pursuit of Excellence."* This is so blatant, that I would like to ask, "Where is the ACLU (American Civil Liberties Union)?" They take up every cause imaginable, but would they dare to be so objective as to take up for the plight of the Christian in the face of such injustice?

Magic Dragon Replaces God in School

FORT MILL, SC - *"When God Leaves, Just Call on Pumsy! Jesus and God can't be with you all the time, so you need to call on Pumsy who will never leave you."* When a guidance counselor told that to a 1st-grader at Fort Mill Primary School, it sparked a big controversy over the New Age curriculum called Pumsy.

When Lori Aldhizer's son, Kyle, came home with Pumsy finger puppets named "Sparkler Mind," "Clear Mind," and "Mud Mind," she became suspicious and began asking him questions. *He said the guidance counselor told the class that, when Jesus and God have to leave you and go somewhere else, you need Pumsy who is the only thing that is with you all the time.*

Pumsy, THE DRAGON, is a character that is supposed to teach children how to think and feel about life situations! He is used in a controversial program used to promote self-esteem which is now being used (according to *San Jose Mercury News*, March 25, 1991), in "more than 12,000 elementary schools nationwide." This cute dragon puppet is used to teach students the art of self-hypnosis. *"Presented as a 'cognitive mental health curriculum,' it trains children to use relaxation exercises, visualizations, and chants to create their own meadow, float through the air on Pumsy's back, meet and speak with Pumsy's friend, feel strength coming into their bodies. . ."* (*Under the Spell of Mother Earth*, Berit Kjos)

When Mr. and Mrs. Aldhizer's son told them what he was learning in school, they knew they had to expose it. They called friends, who then called their friends to spread the news about this strange curriculum. The more the parents learned about the new psychological techniques, the more outraged they became.

They were especially outraged at how Pumsy seemed to open the door for even more problems. **The guidance counselor talked to the children about using crystals and other New Age practices.**

Revelation 20:2 tells us WHO that dragon is and what will happen to him: *"And he laid hold on the dragon, that old serpent, which is the devil, and Satan. . .And cast him into the bottomless pit. . .that he should DECEIVE the nations no more."*

Berit Kjos, in her book *Under the Spell of Mother Earth* cited another entry point of the Mother Goddess into our society via the public school: *"During Earth Day celebrations, children wrote poems to Our Mother, visualized her healing, and used guided IMAGERY to CONNECT with her spirits.* In Brainerd, MN students watched a video titled 'Spaceship Earth: Our Global Environment.' (emphasis ours) In the film, the following shared their beliefs:

"Noel Brown, Director, UN Environment Program: *'We need to develop a better sense of CONNECTEDNESS with all of life.'* (emphasis ours)

"Sting-rock group - 'The Indians believe that the spirits live in the trees..the river..and the air. I think we used to believe that in the past..if there's a spirit in a tree, you don't just chop it down and burn it.'

"Girl - 'I can't separate the destruction of the earth from the destruction of myself..Because we all started out from the earth, we're all going to go back to the earth. The Native Americans called it Mother Earth, and it is.'

Berit continues, "That occult indoctrination can happen on a grand scale was proven during 1989-1990, when teachers in seventy Los Angeles schools introduced children to their personal spirit guides. Two thousand children, third grade and up, participated in the pilot program, *Mission SOAR - 'Set Objectives, Achieve Results.'* Bob Simonds, President of Citizens for Excellence in Education (CEE), alerted parents through a newsletter with the following information:

"'The lessons in Mission SOAR parallel closely. . .the exercises outlined in the New Age book, *Beyond Hypnosis: A Program For Developing Your Psychic and Healing Power,* by leading New Age psychic William H. Hewitt. *Children. . .are hypnotized, introduced to demonic spirits,and told to seek "their counsel" when making decisions.* Hard to Believe?'"

The outline of exercises taught in this program include such steps as, *Conjuring up the dead, summoning spirit guides, creating an inner psychic room to meet spirits, accepting the spirit beings into your life, and receiving psychic power from a white light.*

Al Gore's "spirituality," and Bill Clinton's support of "progressive" education would further this type of educational curriculum. By his stand against private schools and home schooling, he wants to force us to send our children to be indoctrinated into the occult, and against every Christian principle we stand for, and he wants us to finance it.

Further, Clinton is "pro-choice" and just plain "pro" for every special interest group imaginable - except where the Christian principles he claims he champions are involved. He refuses to allow us funds to educate our children in private schools and home schooling environments in order to protect them from this occult onslaught of anti-God occultism in the public schools. **Bill, now is your chance to stand up for God and the Baptist doctrines you say you believe in so wholeheartedly.**

Heretofore, the only separation of church and state, strictly enforced, has been the separation of Bible-believing Christianity and State. As this book clearly reveals, occult religion is blatantly a part of the State school systems, while Christianity is the only religion that is absolutely forbidden.

CAN THEY SAVE THE PARTY?

"CAN THEY SAVE THE PARTY?" queried *U.S. News and World Report*, July 20, 1992 in an article entitled, "Traditional values." "It will not be easy to turn its fortunes around. In the eyes of many, the Democratic Party has become the party of bad economics. It is the party of government at a time when many voters hold government most responsible for the nation's woes. Its association with cultural liberalism has sometimes put it at odds with 'traditional values.'

"Bill Clinton has tried at various points to break with the party orthodoxies that have helped create those problems. Indeed, aides say his selection of Gore was predicated, among other things, on the fact that Gore's wife,

Tipper, is a noted critic of lewd and violent rock lyrics and can help turn back the Republican attacks on Democrats as being "soft on family values."

Bill Clinton has been aware for some time that he must fashion a "new image" if he is to be successful in wooing the American people into giving him a seat in the "Oval Office." This fact was reported in *The Wallstreet Journal*, July 17, 1992: "...Mr. Clinton has spent months (if not years) attempting to fashion himself as a moderate Democrat unwedded to the Big Brother Government programs that have dominated his party for so long, the selection of Al Gore signals a return to yesteryear's agenda. The 1992 Democratic platform may indeed offer a new liberal agenda that rejects "an outdated faith in programs as the solution to every problem." But Mr. Gore's record clearly belies that attitude.

Could the injection of the "spiritual" aspect tie in with what the Bible foretells regarding future events? Clinton repeatedly made reference to the "Scriptures," and we see that the prophetic Scriptures state that a strong religious leader will actually be instrumental in installing a one-world ruler. Revelation 13:12 states that the religious leader, (the false prophet) *"...causeth the earth and them that dwell therein to worship the first beast. . . . "*

Is it any wonder then, that all of a sudden, we are hearing about "spiritual" things - about the "Scriptures?" Is it then strange that we now see a wedding of "spiritual to state?" There is evidently a "spiritual power" that will be useful in promoting political leaders who endorse the spiritual agenda of the new "fundamental neo-paganists."

Of course, there is another strong reason that Clinton and Gore are injecting their own brand of spiritualism into the campaign. The environmental goddess movement (the swing from the oppressive Patriarchal society to the Matriarchal) also ties right in with another movement - the Feminists - and they need them badly, since more women are now voting than men.

CHAPTER EIGHT

THE NEW FEMININE FACE OF "BIG BROTHER"

Power Shift

Quoting again from the *U.S. News and World Report,* the July 20, 1992 article entitled, "Can They Save the Party," it was noted that the business of getting elected has changed. They remarked that one of the striking things was *". . .how drastically power in the party has shifted over a relatively short time."*

In this informative article, Theodore H. White, political analyst, noted that the convention that nominated John Kennedy was dominated by three power blocs: big-city mayors, Southern governors, and labor leaders. "Today, the old urban machines are gone. . . .*Among the major forces at the 1992 convention are women* - or, rather, feminists, since the overwhelming majority of women there share the outlook, attitudes and priorities of the feminist movement. *Women have held half the Democrats' delegate seats since 1980, but they are an increasingly assertive and cohesive bloc.* With the decline of antiwar and antimilitary activism, feminists form the largest bloc of liberal activists. Typically, .55 percent of Democratic primary voters this year were women, and the gender gap that has persisted since 1980 means that more women than men tend to vote Democratic in general elections.

"Women are also increasingly important when it comes to money. 'Every piece of Democratic National Committee direct mail,' say DNC finance director Melissa Moss, mentions "choice," meaning abortion rights. .
.feminist groups have become major Democratic fundraisers. . . . The convention itself is a showcase for women and their causes. In charge of the entire affair is Texas Gov. Ann Richards; the lead off speaker is Maryland Sen. Barbara Mikulski, and women's organizations will dominate the prime outside-the-hall events and social gatherings.

"On the issues side, the rising authority of women is even more striking. While Clinton refused to endorse labor's litmus-test positions, declined to back the Democratic mayors' urban aid wish list and publicly scuffled with Jesse Jackson, he took care to support the Freedom of Choice Act on abortion even though it seemed to prohibit the sort of parental notification he signed into law in Arkansas. And he promised to 'run a pro-choice campaign with a pro-choice ticket.'

". . .pro-abortion-rights groups in 1992 are trying to move Democrats to oppose all restrictions on abortion."

Is the picture beginning to take shape?

Quoting again the paragraph from page 260 of *Earth in the Balance, we see Gore's swing from a* "patriarchal" view to a "matriarchal" *spiritual experience.*

Christianity vs the Goddess

"A growing number of anthropologists and archaeo-*MYTHOLOGISTS*, such as Marija Gimbutas and Rian Eisler, argue that the prevailing ideology of belief in prehistoric Europe and much of the world was based on the worship of A SINGLE EARTH GODDESS, who was assumed to be the fount of all life and who radiated harmony among all living things...the evidence for the existence of this primitive RELIGION comes from the many 1000's of artifacts uncovered in ceremonial sites. *THESE SITES ARE SO WIDESPREAD THAT THEY SEEM TO CONFIRM THE NOTION THAT A GODDESS RELIGION WAS UBIQUITOUS* throughout much of the world UNTIL the antecedents of TODAY'S religions - *most of which still have a DISTINCTLY MASCULINE ORIENTATION* - almost obliterating belief in the goddess. The last vestige of *ORGANIZED GODDESS WORSHIP WAS ELIMINATED BY CHRISTIANITY* as late as the 15th century in Lithuania...the archaeological scholarship is impressive, and it seems obvious THAT A *better understanding of a religious heritage preceding our own by so many 1000's of years could offer us new insights into the nature of the human experience.* [EMPHASIS OURS]

Does this begin to fit into the PC Feminist agenda? Let's examine the feminist agenda at the Earth summit. According to Berit Kjos, "The feminist arm of the Earth Summit blends all four pillars of the green colossus: Marxist idealism (and oppression), an illusion of peace, earth-centered spirituality, and a feminist agenda. So when the World Women's Congress gathered 1500 women from 83 countries last November to prepare a plan for *the Earth Summit, the opening prayers for the assembly did not address the Creator. Instead, spiritist Madonna Blue Horse Beard led the assembly in a pagan assortment of chants, meditations and prayers to the spirits of the earth - all manifestations of a pantheistic earth goddess.* Chairwoman Bella Abzug, former U.S. Congresswoman, introduced an African choir. But *when they sang praises to God, Abzug cried into the microphone, "You mean the goddess!"* (Reported by Jean Guilfoyle, Director of International Studies, Human Life International, Gaithersburg, MD)

"The most anguished voices at the Congress came from Third World women ravaged by the coercive population control technologies of the United Nations Population Fund and Planned Parenthood. Their grievances were voiced but ignored, buried by Western feminists to whom choice meant, not individual choice, but that everyone must bend to their choice to heal the earth through oppressive, compulsory controls. No wonder, God's Word shows that when people turn from God to paganism, justice dies and pain multiplies.

"Earth Summit leader Maurice Strong has vowed to endorse and promote the *"Women's Agenda 21"* which *includes issues such as gender balance*, women-managed reproductive health care, demilitarization, and universal environmental education. The latter fits right into Strong's own beliefs. He is member of the Baha'i World Faith, which proclaims the unity of all religions [into his own], the oneness of all people, and the coming of "A Promised One" - a manifestation of God who would unify all his followers. Strong appropriately calls his New Age ranch and study center in Colorado "The Valley of the Refuge of World Truths." (**E magazine**, May/June 1992)"

CHAPTER NINE

RADICAL ENVIRONMENTALISM SCIENCE - "FALSELY SO-CALLED"

CLINTON, GORE - PRODUCTS OF THE '60s

From the Counter Culture to the Earth Summit

"At our universities during the sixties, four overlapping anti- establishment groups joined to form the green movement: Radical feminists, Marxist (the New Left), peace-niks (the anti-war movement), and hippies seeking spiritual enlightenment. Since their common foes were Western culture and Christian values, many sought answers to earthly problems in Eastern spirituality, earth-centered rituals, and a utopian vision of global equality.

"The philosophical blend that shaped the student movement of the sixties now reaches around the world. Its labels have changed but not its goals. Listen to the voices of the environmental leaders of the world as they gathered in Brazil on June 1 for the United Nations Earth Summit (UNCED). Instead of world-wide Marxism, they proclaim the need for "eradicating poverty" through a global welfare system controlled by environmentalists and financed by the West. Instead of protesting the Vietnam War, they now battle the "oppressive patriarchal" mentality that supposedly opened the door to current abuses and severed our relationship to nature. Instead of psychedelic drugs, they seek spiritual insights through tribal wisdom and pantheistic connectedness. Christianity is out. In its place has risen a nurturing, harmonious, all-inclusive Mother Earth spirituality designed for the nineties. All religions fit under its broad umbrella - except Biblical Christianity." (Berit Kjos)

Gore Calls for Global Marshall Plan and Strategic Environmental Initiative

Although the press has scrambled to portray Mr. Gore as an environmental "moderate," a close look shows he is quite radical. *"Mr. Gore has called for a 'Global Marshall Plan' and a 'Strategic Environmental Initiative' designed to save the world from ecological destruction. Anything short of total war in this effort is appeasement,* 'designed to satisfy the public's desire to believe that wrenching transformation of society will not be necessary.' (*The Wallstreet Journal,* July 17, 1992)

According to this same issue of *The Wallstreet Journal,* "The outline of Mr. Gore's radical environmental vision is found in his book, *'Earth in the Balance:*

Ecology and the Human Spirit (Houghton Mifflin, 1992). The best seller charges 'we must make the rescue of the environment the central organizing principle for civilization.' Mr. Gore actually researched and wrote this book himself. All the more reason to fear the environmental policies that might result from a Clinton-Gore administration.

The Wrong Answers

According to leading authorities, despite all the research Gore did on the environment for his book, he has somehow come up with the wrong answers. Everyone is entitled to make mistakes, but when you see the price Mr. Gore's misleading assumptions and anti-Christian solutions would extract from unwary American people, it becomes criminal.

"Unfortunately, Mr. Gore, like much of the environmental establishment, gets the scientific evidence wrong on the threats facing the earth's ecology. Consider his views on global warming, which is to Mr. Gore 'the most dangerous of all' environmental threats. As writers including Fred S. Singer have noted. . .the data have yet to support such a conclusion. Moreover, surveys of scientists, conducted by Gallup, and even Greenpeace, disprove Mr. Gore's claim that 98% of scientists support his fears. *Mr. Gore credits Roger Revelle for alerting him to the danger global warming poses, yet Revelle himself wrote that 'The scientific* *base for a greenhouse warming is too uncertain to justify drastic action at this time.'*

"Because of the grave threat he sees on the horizon, Mr. Gore calls for a vast array of new laws and expanded bureaucracies to preserve the earth's ecological balance. Thus Mr. Gore wholeheartedly endorsed the green internationalist agenda unveiled at the Rio Earth Summit, **COMPLETE WITH MASSIVE REDISTRIBUTION OF WEALTH** in developing nations. In this posture he "outgreened" President Bush, who pledged almost $900 million, but failed to sign off on the most redistributionist proposals put forward in Rio. (emphasis ours) *(The Wallstreet Journal, July 17,1992)*

"Calling the. . .Rio Earth Summit a 'charade' and claiming its real objective is to 'consolidate enormous power in the hands of Green bureaucrats at the United Nations,' *CFACT* Executive Director Craig J. Rucker today urged U.S. leaders 'not to jeopardize the future of our nation or our world by signing the costly and destructive environmental treaties. . .proposed in Brazil.' *He also charged the environmental movement with hyping such unproven doomsday theories as global warming, species extinction, and ozone depletion as a way to scare countries into voluntarily relinquishing much of their national sovereignty.*

A Global Green Empire

"Rucker explained THE EARTH SUMMIT WILL ACCOMPLISH THE LONG- SOUGHT GOAL OF ESTABLISHING A 'GLOBAL GREEN EMPIRE' BY GIVING THE U.N. THE FUNDS AND AUTHORITY TO EFFECTIVELY BECOME A SINGE WORLD GOVERNMENT. 'If Greens succeed at Rio,' he asserted, 'their friends in *the U.N. will be able to extort huge sums of cash from developed countries, decide how the world's resources will be divvied-up, and keep the Third World chained to their new international welfare system.* It's no wonder the meeting's chairman, Maurice Strong, said he expects the summit to 'change the behavior not only of government but of individuals everywhere,' Rucker added.

Transfer of Wealth - Economic Disaster

"Concerning the summit's impact on U.S. citizens, Rucker said **Rio could wreak economic havoc throughout the developed world. 'Monstrous transfer payments, new energy taxes, and environmental surcharges will cost us countless jobs and literally trillions of dollars,'** he stated, 'and I expect our standard-of-living will suffer immeasurably. He also affirmed the Earth Summit will be disastrous for the Third World since it will 'penalize any meaningful progress and prohibit developing countries from using safe technologies to feed and care for their starving masses.

"All of this sacrifice would almost be tolerable if we were actually facing an impending ecological Armageddon,' Rucker concluded, but the only ones the Earth Summit will benefit are the ideologues willing to exploit the environment for their own selfish purposes." (May 6, 1992 *CFACT* press release)

How "strong" are the convictions of Earth Summit leader, Strong's convictions? In an article entitled, "Controversial Summit Leader, Millionaire believes profit, planetary survival can go hand in hand." from the June 2, 1992 issue of *The Wallstreet Journal*, we find the following report: ". . . .there are some who see in Strong, not the perfect marriage of profit and planetary survival but of their irreconcilable differences.

"Nowhere is that view more pronounced than in the San Luis Valley in the high desert of southern Colorado, where *a company founded by Strong wants to pump precious water from the ground and sell it to thirsty cities like Denver and Los Angeles. . . .It would just devastate the whole area.*

"Locals are worried that the plan will draw on the valley's natural underground reservoir, forcing farmers out of business and desiccating prime wetlands. . . .

"It would turn us into another Owens Valley," whose water was taken early in the century to build subdivisions near Los Angeles, said Kizzen Dennet, editor of the monthly paper in Crestone, a town of about 300 near the

100,000 acre Baca ranch where the company wants to sink its wells.

"'You've got to give the man credit for what he's doing (at the Earth Summit),' said Dennett. 'But Maurice Strong is not very popular here in San Luis Valley.'

"Although Strong withdrew from the project shortly before being named secretary-general of the U.N. parley, he reportedly retained a small royalty interest (to be donated to charity), and the company, American Water Development, Inc., is pressing ahead with its plans.

"Strong's Danish wife, Hanne, meanwhile, lives year-round at Baca ranch and pursues a different sort of development - spiritual.

"The two have donated money and land to create a desert mecca of sorts for a variety of traditional and New Age orders. *There is a Zen center, a Carmelite hermitage and a Tibetan monastery. Actress Shirley McLaine is said to be among the spiritual seekers who own a piece of the pinon-dotted ranch."*

I am still trying to figure out which of these orders are "traditional."

The Devil's Horsemen Ride Again

Quoting from *Citizen Outlook*, May/June 1992, "When Genghis Kahn's 'Devil's Horsemen' thundered out of

Kharakorum on their way to conquering one medieval kingdom after another, when Napoleon stunned the crowd at Paris' Notre Dame Cathedral by snatching the crown away from Pope Pious VII and proclaiming himself King of France, and when Hitler sent waves of Panzer tanks blitzing across the plains of Poland to establish his Thousand Year Reich, the dream of global domination was foremost in each of their thoughts.

"While it is easy to relegate such lust for world power to the dusty pages of history, *this same ambition is alive and well today - and can be found among the leaders of the world's environmental movement. Although garbed in Armani suits instead of battle armor and firing-off press releases rather than artillery rounds, these ideologues are not less hungry for world predominance than their ruthless predecessors. The. . .Earth Summit in Rio de Janiero is their boldest attempt yet to create a global Green Empire."* (emphasis ours)

They state that signing these agreements will "move [the environment] into the center of economic policy and decision making. . . .By whipping the world into a frenzy with constant reports of an impending ecological Armageddon, countries are being seduced into voluntarily surrendering their autonomy to the UN."

The fact is, the environmental dangers so loudly touted, have yet to be proven conclusively. We have heard so many varying stories on the "Greenhouse Effect" that it is like the weather man's predictions - "maybe, maybe not." *"Abstract data. . .is virtually all global warming theorists have to go on since little or no confidence can be placed in the actual temperature record. . . .*

If you recall the article previously quoted regarding the bias of the media on the environment, there was *quite a number of scientists who disagree with the catastrophic projections of environmentalists* - but they were mysteriously missing from the speakers list at the media sponsored conferences.

"First, the Earth's temperature is constantly changing. When dinosaurs ruled the land, the planet's average temperature was estimated to be 15 degrees F hotter than it is today. And when our landscapes and lakes were carved by Ice Ages that routinely occur. . .no one was sunbathing at the Jersey shore. Radical temperature changes have simply taken place throughout history and are not reliant on jammed freeways or billowing factories." (*Citizen Outlook*, July/August 1991.)

"Palm trees on the Potomac, a dust bowl in the Midwest, coastal cities under water, and Anchorage scorched by desert heat. Such are the predictions of those clamoring to avert the horrors of global warming. But are these warnings legitimate or merely a smokescreen for another agenda? Mounting evidence has convinced may scientists the greenhouse theory is just a lot of hot air.

"*With more questions than answers about global warming, it is remarkable that anyone would use this theory to advocate the complete restructuring of our world economy.* This, however, is exactly what environmental extremists are doing. . . .it is also not surprising that the "greenhouse crisis," with its global ramifications, enables the movement to fulfill its perennial dream of environmental regulation." (*Citizen Outlook*, July/August 1991)

There is now evidence that chloroflurocarbons, CFCs, are not the only culprit for the depletion in the ozone, in fact, only about 10% of the depletion can be attributed to CFCs. Scientists are now saying the weakening and expansion of earth's magnetic field has caused the ozone to dissipate. Since the remedies proposed by Al Gore and other radical environmentalists are so drastic, can we at least wait until the evidence is in? Must we rush headlong into a worse disaster just on "theory?" Of course, it seems that the environment is not the real agenda anyway - is it?

The Great American Robbery

In his radical plan to save the environment, "MR. GORE WISHES TO EXPORT CAPITAL RATHER THAN CAPITALISM, to the Third World." (emphasis ours) (*The Wallstreet Journal*, July 17, 1992) *Export capital? Does that include mine? And yours? YES! Redistribute the world's wealth? Does this mean give U.S. wealth to the Third World? YES! Does this mean the "dismantling of America" as we know it? YES!*

Does this begin to sound a bit familiar? Are we seeing the true image of Al Gore begin to subtly emerge? When we look at all the other liberal New Agers now in our government and in positions of power, they still pale in comparison to the radical agenda Al Gore has in mind for you and for me.

Mr. Gore's radical environmental proposals would put hundreds of thousands of people out of work. They would drive up the price of goods to the point that our lifestyles would be hardly recognizable. Projections are that just one of Gore's proposals to tax carbon would mean an increase of 26 cents per gallon of gasoline, and coal prices would more than double. This information was taken from a study conducted by the Department of Energy.

The Road Back to Serfdom

Quoting from an article by Fred L. Smith, *The Wallstreet Journal*, July 17, 1992: "...Mr. Gore is a true product of the 1960s. Then political intellectuals were on the vanguard of economic central planning. The "best and the brightest," we were told, would find a way to eliminate poverty, flatten the business cycle and fine-tune the economy into full employment and rapid economic growth. The result was an utter disaster. If Mr. Gore remains true to his own past, he will want to replicate these central planning mistakes under an ecological banner. The road to serfdom need not be paved with red bricks: Green bricks will do just fine.

"It is worth mentioning here that the danger of Mr. Gore's agenda is not confined to massive environmental programs. **The National Taxpayers Union has consistently ranked Mr. Gore as one of the Senate's biggest spenders; Mr. Gore topped their list in 1989 and 1990.**"

Senator Malthus

The Wall Street Journal calls Gore, "Senator Malthus." In an article in the August 3, 1992 issue they point out that "The air in American cities is cleaner than 20 years ago, once dead rivers and lakes are now safe for fishing and many endangered species are again abundant. Yet Al Gore. . .says we're headed for an 'ecological Kristallnacht.' We think there is a debate to be joined here in this election year.

"Kristallnacht was the night-time Nazi rampage of Jews in the 1930s. Other Germans heard the screams and saw the shattered glass but did nothing. Mr. Gore thinks Americans who aren't changing their lives to solve the 'grave crisis' of the environment are on par with Germans who let Jews go to the gas chamber.

"Now anyone can get carried away once in a while, even us. But in the case of Senator Gore, such rhetoric has become standard issue. He's even collected his apocalyptic thoughts into a 1992 book, '*Earth in the Balance: Ecology and the Human Spirit.*'

"The book deserves nationwide circulation because it so passionately takes one side of the argument over how to maintain economic growth and protect the environment. Mr. Gore is part of a tradition going back to the famous 17th century economist Thomas Robert Malthus. At the cusp of that great burst of prosperity known as the industrial revolution, Malthus argued that population growth would inevitably outstrip food supply, leading to famine and war.

The Disassembling of America

"Naturally, looming catastrophe demands radical solutions. Mr. Gore wants a "strategic environment initiative" (SEI) that would use the tax code and regulation to phase out "old technologies," whatever those might be. One apparently is the car. "Within the context of SEI, it ought to be possible to establish a coordinated global program to accomplish the strategic goal of completely eliminating the internal combustion engine over, say, a 25 year period," he writes.

"He wants a 'Global Marshall Plan' of at least $100 billion to pay for much of this. And he'd 'require the wealthy nations' - that means us - 'to allocate money for transferring environmentally helpful technologies to the Third World.' Someone should ask Bill Clinton if he agrees with this.

"We don't belittle the urge for a cleaner earth, nor the yearning for a cause greater than material wealth. But our own view of history differs from Mr. Gore's. We see economic progress as a prerequisite to environmental cleanup. And the surest path to economic progress is not strategic plans or global taxes or technology transfer to Third World kleptocrats; It is the genius of liberated minds and markets.

"IT'S NO ACCIDENT THAT THE CLEANEST LAKES ARE NOW IN THE WEALTHY FREE-MARKET WEST, WHILE THE WORST POLLUTION IS IN BEIJING OR RUSSIA'S ARAL SEA. IF SOMEONE IS GOING TO FIND A WAY TO REDUCE 'GLOBAL WARMING' ASSUMING SCIENCE ONE DAY SHOWS THAT TO BE DESIRABLE , HE WON'T BE EMPLOYED BY SOME GLOBAL EPA."
(EMPHASIS OURS)

Berit Kjos gives the Biblical view of what environmental protection should be based on in order to succeed. "Only an awakening to the Creator of the earth, not to paganism of universalism, can bring genuine healing. God told His people to trust Him and care for His beautiful creation. With this responsibility, He also gave us the capacity to know His heart and be led by His Spirit. The key to earth-stewardship is oneness with the heart and mind of the Creator Himself, not the counterfeit oneness of pantheism. When we view nature through His loving eyes, care for it with His sensitive wisdom, and allow its beauty to point us to the greatness of its Maker, He will enable His people and bless His land."

SUMMARY

Beloved, out of the ashes of personal tragedy, Gore has emerged *as the legendary Phoenix, a new and transformed creature.* He renounces the beliefs of his "Baptist" heritage, "For some Christians the prophetic vision of the apocalypse is used - *IN MY VIEW UNFORGIVABLY* (emphasis ours)." Then the New Gore steps forward to unveil his "Global Marshall Plan" for mankind.

The least of our worries are summed up in the economic proposals Gore makes. These, alone, would put hundreds of thousands of people out of work. They would drive up the price of goods to the point that our lifestyles would be hardly recognizable (*including a carbon tax proposal that would increase the price of gas by 26 cents per gallon*), and export American capital to Third World countries in a redistribution of the earth's wealth. But *the most ominous threat of all is the "spiritual" transformation he would impose upon us - thereby DESTROYING OUR RELIGIOUS FREEDOM!*

The consequences that would come from the leadership of a person holding the neo-pagan fundamentalist agenda of Al Gore, are horrendous. His nihilistic philosophy, akin to the shambles witnessed in Russia. The accompanying results of that philosophy, are profoundly addressed in the first chapter of Romans.

The Bible identifies the type of people referred to in this chapter in verse 25. They are a group of people who have *"exchanged the truth of God for the lie - and worshipped and served the creature* (the pantheistic beliefs of Al Gore - the worship of the earth as the Mother Goddess and the neo-pagan tenets of the "deep ecologists") *more than the Creator, who is blessed forever. Amen.*

Beloved, the catastrophic consequences that befall a people who give themselves over to such perversions are described in Romans 1:17-32. We are already experiencing many of the judgments outlined in this text because of the inroads this neo-pagan fundamentalist ideology has already made into every facet of our society.

WHAT CAN WE DO?

We CAN do something. God wants us to present our bodies a living sacrifice unto Him, that He might reveal Himself through us. Matthew 5:13 tells us, *"Ye are the salt of the earth: but if the salt has lost his savor, wherewith shall it be salted? it is thenceforth good for nothing, but to be cast out."*

Some concerned parents in our hometown of Broken Arrow, Oklahoma, have recently won a tremendous battle in our town. The *Earth Child* pilot curriculum that we described in this book was being sponsored in our school system, by the Public Service Company of Oklahoma. Broken Arrow parents objecting to the neo-pagan "ancient religious rituals and mental games," "salted" PSO with their concerns about the curriculum in letters, calls and through the local media. PSO corporate community services manager recently announced that *"Earth Child"* books and training workshops for teachers, childcare providers and others will no longer be provided to schools or other organizations by PSO.

As parents, grandparents, aunts, uncles and fellow citizens, let's join hands and hearts in standing together in defeating the "big lie" that is such an ominous threat to our religious freedom. If allowed to continue, unthwarted, this neo-pagan fundamentalist movement will ultimately deprive all of us of our "choice" of religious persuasion and practice.

The Bible informs us in II Thessalonians 2:7-8 that we, who are indwelt by the Spirit of Jesus Christ, are to serve as a restraint against the mystery of lawlessness and not allow it's full power to overcome the world. Let us go forward in *"proclaiming the truth in love, and loving the truth we proclaim."*

For Free FRONTPAGE Newspaper

John Barela publishes a current events monthly news-
paper, *FRONTPAGE*. It will keep you abreast of the
latest events and issues confronting us TODAY, examine
them in light of THE BIBLE, and show how they affect
YOU and your family.

If you would like to receive a subscription to this
information- packed 16 page newsletter, absolutely free,
please write to:

FRONTPAGE
10977 East 23rd Street
Tulsa, OK 74129

OTHER VALUABLE BOOKS

THE COMING HOLOCAUST
IN THE MIDDLE EAST:

Desert Storm, Phase 2

by John Barela

- *Have we heard the last from Saddam?*
- *Has the Middle East now become a "POWDER KEG" waiting for a "madman" to light the fuse?*

Find out how the current "hidden agenda" of the New World Order fits hand-In-glove with *THE COMING HOLOCAUST IN THE MIDDLE EAST.*

John Barela "unlocks" formerly obscure Bible passages to give us the most startling prophetic scenario since "The Late Great Planet Earth." This information is fresh and new - you will not read it in any other book on Bible prophecy. *THE COMING HOLOCAUST IN THE MIDDLE EAST* is "must" reading for every Christian - even if you have never studied Bible prophecy before!

Order your copy of *THE COMING HOLOCAUST IN THE MIDDLE EAST* today.

1 copy for $10
3 copies for $25
Video tape Part 1 for $25, Part 2 for $25 or both for $40
Audio cassette series $12